2.99

(10)

The Peculiar People

The Peculiar People

by
Mark Sorrell

EXETER
THE PATERNOSTER PRESS

AUSTRALIA:
Emu Book Agencies Pty., Ltd.,
63, Berry St., Granville, 2142, N.S.W.

SOUTH AFRICA:
Oxford University Press,
P.O. Box 1141, Cape Town

British Library Cataloguing in Publication Data

Sorrell, Mark
    The Peculiar People.
    1. Union of Evangelical Churches – History
    I. Title
    289.9   BX8750.P43

    ISBN: 0 85364 263 X

Typeset by Input Typesetting Ltd, London and printed and bound in Great Britain by Redwood Burn Limited, Trowbridge and Esher for The Paternoster Press Ltd, Paternoster House, 3 Mount Radford Crescent, Exeter, Devon.

Contents

List of Illustrations

Foreword

I confess I had never heard of the Peculiar People until I became the minister of a church in Essex. I then discovered that in different parts of the county there were chapels, apparently well attended which belonged to a denomination known as The Peculiar People.

Some years later I met the young lady who was to become my wife only to find she belonged to this body of Christians. Through her I learned a good deal about The Peculiar People. Her grandfather was Bishop William Heddle, and her immediate family were active in the chapel at Stanway near Colchester. I gained the impression that the services at Stanway were very lively, making a particular appeal to young people. I found that some of the chapels were more old-fashioned in their outlook and attitudes than others. There were still women who wore quaint Quakerish dress with black bonnets!

As I pieced things together I gained a fair picture of The Peculiar People. They clearly had a zeal for evangelism. They believed in liberty in worship and did not have a paid ministry. The most significant feature of the Peculiar People however was their reluctance to call on the services of the medical profession in cases of illness. This fact often gave them unwelcome publicity in the popular press. Before long I met the venerable Bishop himself – physically a diminutive figure yet a man of strong convictions. He was somewhat patriarchal, calling his large family together from time to time for "family gatherings". William Heddle had been married twice. There were three children from his first marriage and ten from the second so a family gathering was quite an occasion! One such gathering took place in Southend on 12th August 1946 when all the Heddle family were invited by "great grandpa and great grandma" "to attend a family gathering of Thanksgiving to commemorate great grandpa's 100th birthday". The family at that time was closely knit and relatives came from near and far to honour the head of the family.

William Heddle was undoubtedly an astute business man. He set up his sons with businesses of their own and passed on to them something of his own business acumen. His standards were puritanical. He was also a man of great generosity although he was always careful to see that his gifts went to causes in which he had absolute confidence. If any suspicion arose as to the conduct of the affairs of any society which he had been supporting, he had no hesitation in cutting off his support summarily!

In some ways The Peculiar People were an anachronism and yet in a sense they led the way for the charismatic movement of our time. Their services were not dissimilar to those of many Pentecostal groups today. It is to their credit that they came to terms with reality and recognised that their very name was an embarrassment to them and so they had the courage to change it. Although they have always held tenaciously to their faith, the "peculiars" have not been guilty, at least as far I have known them, of being unco-operative in supporting other evangelical Christians. They have been pleased to back whole-heartedly united evangelistic campaigns and conventions.

In a sense when they lost their original name they lost their distinctive identity, but the cause of Christ would be much the poorer without the "union of evangelical churches" as they are now known.

I for one am glad to think that their story is finding its way into print, and I believe the account we have is both factual, well documented and fascinating to read.

GILBERT A. KIRBY

Acknowledgements

I am glad to have been able to write the history of The Peculiar People, and I thank all those who have helped to make this possible.

I am especially grateful to the following: Mr Martyn Anderson; Mr E. A. Barnes; Mr Horace Belsham; Mrs F. Bolton; Mrs Joan E. Brandon; Mr E. W. Brazier; Mrs Pearl Bright; Mrs Lillian Cooper and Mrs Ruby Whipps; Mr F. Costen; Mrs Rebecca Freeman; Mrs M. Gibson; Miss G. M. Godbold; Mr and Mrs Hallpike; Mrs Frances Hayman; Mr Ernest Hockley; Mr and Mrs Jesse Horsnell; Mr James Howson (Curator/Archivist at Barking Libraries); Mr Arthur C. Larke; Mrs Edna McCarthy; Mr Dennis Morgan of "The Southend Standard"; Mrs T. Mortimer; Mr Aubrey Rayner; Mr Mark Spicer; Mrs Dinah M. Steel; Mr George Thorington; Mrs Lydia West; Miss Joan Whitwell; Mr and Mrs E. Whale; Mr Andrew Wood.

My thanks to all of these; and to Messrs C. C. Wiggins, W. Whale, and S. J. Thorn of the Union of Evangelical Churches for reading the manuscript and suggesting improvements; to Mr George Tanner, my uncle, and Mr John Wood, for printing old photographs kindly lent to me.

Above all, I wish to acknowledge here my great and special debt to Mr Frank Smith, retired minister of Eastwood Evangelical Church and a lifelong member, for all his help in unravelling the complex history of the People. Mr Smith's researches, and information generously supplied by him, have done much to shape this book; and the final, retrospective chapter (Chapter Six) is by him.

CHAPTER I

Enthusiasm in the Nineteenth Century

"The Peculiar People" was the name given to a religious sect that flourished in Essex and neighbouring counties, in the nineteenth and twentieth centuries. Few in numbers and obscure to fame, the Peculiars yet gained a more than local reputation about the turn of the century for their practice of divine healing, and for their refusal to allow their children to be attended by doctors in times of sickness. When deaths, court cases and terms of imprisonment revealed the presence of this religion to a wider public, secular opinion set hard against it, and the rationalists of that age dismissed it as one more brand of religious fanaticism. The circumstances of this opposition, the lives of the Peculiars, and the subsequent history of the sect (for, though under another name, it continues to this day), with other articles of interest, form the subject of this book.

The founder of the Peculiar People, James Banyard, was a ploughman's son, born on the 31st January 1800, in the small market town of Rochford, in south-east Essex (see sketch map on page 00). Rochford, on the River Roach, lies on the edge of a marshland region that extends up the east coast of Essex. It is now almost incorporated into the sprawl of Southend: there is an airfield nearby and a large hospital. In Banyard's youth, it consisted of a collection of 180 houses disposed along four roads – North, South, East and West Streets – about a market-square, and was surrounded by great fields of corn. The whole of Essex was given over to agriculture: it was, with the other eastern counties, the corn garner of England. It was, however, singularly lacking in great houses and great estates, at least in the southern part.

Its politics were conservative, its religion earnestly nonconformist, a bastion of the Puritan cause from Elizabethan
times. The Peculiar People were to prove that, even in the
nineteenth century, Puritanism and religious controversy
were not dead there.

James Banyard worked on the land, like his father before
him. He was a man of "quick natural parts". "Had he been
an educated man," wrote one clergyman, "there is reason to
think that he would have occupied a good position in
society". Like that of Bunyan, his early youth was disreput-
able. His chief companion is described as one William Layzell
(alias Jack Ketch), formerly a smuggler. His chief resorts
were public houses and local fairs. He amused himself by
composing and singing glees and popular songs, also burl-
esques of his neighbours, copies of which he would sell in
the streets. He is said to have diverted his companions by
scattering peas on the steps of one of the Nonconformist
chapels in the town. He excelled in conjuring tricks and
mimicry, and drew considerable company into the public
houses of the district with his human and animal imperson-
ations. So conscientious was he in perfecting an imitation of
an horse's mouth by pulling out his lips, that he is said to
have permanently deformed himself: this tomfoolery,
according to a later witness, made him "the ugliest man I
ever saw"[1]. At one point in his youth, he was convicted of
poaching and sent to prison, where he learnt the trade of
shoemaker, by which industry he subsequently earned his
living.

He married one Susan Garnish, but his intemperate habits
continued and were the despair of his wife. At length, however in his early thirties,[2] he saw the error of his ways. A
sudden change came over him. After visiting the fair at
Paglesham, a village a mile or two from Rochford, where
he spent all he had, and even parted with some of his clothing, he was most wretched, and promised his wife that on
the following Sunday he would attend the local Wesleyan
chapel. This he did, and impressed with what he had heard
there, he joined the Wesleyan body, soon becoming a zealous
local preacher. At the same time, he turned decisively from
alcohol, and became a strict teetotaller. The full extent of his
change of heart may be gauged from a witticism of his that

circulated the neighbourhood at the time: "If you want to get me to a public house", the reformed Jack Banyard is reported to have said, "you'll have to take a horse and hook me"[3].

In 1837, William Bridges, a hat block maker from London, arrived in Rochford, on a visit to his sister who lived in the town. Like Banyard, he was a devout Wesleyan preacher, and the two men soon met and had much talk together, some of which was about teetotalism. When William Bridges left Rochford, he invited Banyard to London, promising to supply him with books and other information about tee-totalism, which had not as yet become a principle of Methodism. The zealous Banyard went soon afterwards to London to see his friend. William Bridges met him with a surprising story:

> Glory be to God, James (he said) I have found something better than teetotalism, since I saw you. God has made a blessed change in my soul; He has baptised me with the Holy Ghost, which has quite changed my nature, and made me holy and happy in His love, and removed all my doubts and fears. Bless God, there is no fear in love, no doubts in believers, no sin in Christians. I have been to hear Mr Ankin, who used to be a church clergyman, but the Spirit of God moved him to dissent. He is gifted to show professors (nominal Christians) their empty state. At the time I heard him he preached from the fifth chapter of Genesis, and the 24th verse: "Enoch walked with God", and said that nothing short of this was true religion. I felt by what he said that all I had got was of no use. I knew that I did not begin right, but as I believed Christ bought salvation for me, I could not rest until I found it. By believing that Christ bore away all my sins, I found life and liberty to my soul[4].

James Banyard was astonished at this, but admired the change that had obviously been wrought in his friend. In fact, Bridges had been to hear Robert Aitken (not Ankin), a powerful preacher from the north of England, who had recently hired a hall for preaching at White's Row, Holborn, a few streets away from where Bridges lived, at No 8 Gravel Lane. Aitken[5], had indeed left the Church of England, in 1834, after the tone of some of his sermons had incurred the displeasure of his superior, the Bishop of Chester. He had then begun to preach among the Methodists at Liverpool but, not being in entire agreement with them, had set off on his own through England, on a roving commission, expounding his own doctrine. He preached Methodism in its original simplicity, and chiefly and with great force, the principle of the 'rebirth' of the sinner into Christ, an experience that, fully undergone in faith, purges and presents the believer to the world as one new-washed, free from guilt and sin. It is a reflection on the state of Methodism at the time, that Bridges, a Methodist preacher, should receive this fundamental doctrine of his faith from Aitken as a revelation, and that Banyard in his turn should be similarly moved by it.

Banyard stayed with his friend for several days, and during that time they attended some meetings together. When Banyard saw the joyful, happy state of William Bridges, he began to be assailed by doubts such as Bridges had previously experienced, and to wonder if he too were not a mere formalist in religion. Doubts grew into a conviction of unworthiness, the comforts of his faith slipped from him one by one, and he felt himself undone. On the morning when he was about to leave London, he said to Bridges, in grief and sorrow, "How can I go home like this and tell them (meaning his congregation), that I have had no religion?" Bridges pitied him, and said, "Go up into my bedchamber and ask the Lord to help you". Banyard went back into the house, and fell on his knees in an upstairs room. And there, according to the accounts, while praying he was "born again" and heard the voice of God speaking to him in the words of Jeremiah 15:19–21:

> Therefore thus saith the Lord, if thou return, then I will bring thee again, and thou shalt stand before me; and if thou take forth the precious from the vile thou shalt be as my mouth: let them return unto thee, but return not thou unto them.
> And I will make thee unto the people a fenced brazen wall: and they shall fight against thee, but they shall not prevail against thee: for I am with thee to save thee and deliver thee, saith the Lord.
> And I will deliver thee out of the hand of the wicked, and I will redeem thee out of the hand of the terrible.

This was the crucial experience of Banyard's life. These words and the experience of the 'rebirth' convinced him that

Right: *William Bridges of London (see p. 15)*

(see p. 15)

Below: *James Banyard's Grave in Rochford churchyard. (The stone dates from the 1950's.)*

"THE PECULIAR PEOPLE"

Will (D.V.) **OPEN**

Castle Cottage

Near foot of CHURCH HILL,

Leigh-on-Sea,

FOR

PUBLIC WORSHIP

ON

THE LORD'S DAY,

August 8th, 1915,

at 6.30 p.m.

A Cordial Invitation to All

To Come and Hear the Gospel of the Grace
of God,

How YOU may be SAVED and know
your Sins forgiven.

Come and Hear.   *All Seats Free.*

D. Reeves, Printer, 23 Victoria Avenue, Southend.

*Chapel Bill, Leigh,
1915*

he had been made an agent of God's work, a missionary divinely appointed to restore the true religion. They gave him courage and confidence in the difficult days ahead; they raised him to a peak of exaltation in the knowledge of the rightness of his cause.

Now he was ready and eager to set off, for it was in the timeless, flat, marsh-and-field landscape of his boyhood and youth, rather than here in busy London, that Banyard conceived that his work must be done. Just as he was about to start, William Bridges asked him if he wanted the books about teetotalism, but Banyard replied, "No, no, praise God! I have got something far better", and the two friends rejoiced together.

Banyard returned to Rochford a new man, and took his place among the Wesleyans. He was a bold and fearless man, and, "like the apostle Paul for zeal", it is said, he at once began his mission. He preached his own experience of elemental Methodism: that there is no sin in Christians, no doubts in believers. That we must be born again and receive the Holy Ghost from heaven, for to know our sins are really forgiven is the first step in religion. This doctrine made a great stir among the Rochford congregation. The shining eyes, the confident voice, the fiery evangelistic message were not what they had been used to, even from their old James Banyard, and the majority were made most unhappy by it. Some said he had been to London and had come home crazy, and that they could not have their brethren upset and themselves condemned. Others said it was just the thing they required if they wished to get to heaven, but the church leaders were against him, and sought to be rid of him.

Banyard's ministry with the Wesleyans came to an end one Sunday evening after his return from London, when he announced that he intended to hold a prayer meeting in the chapel on the following night, a break with the normal Methodist practice at that date. The Deacon, a Mr D. Cook, led the revolt, exclaiming (it is said): "Not here:" "Then", Banyard answered him, "At my house, for all who wish to come!" He left, and seventeen of his congregation left with him.

Regular meetings began to be held in Banyard's cramped cottage in West Street. Not content with this modest success,

he took to preaching out of doors – the practice had lapsed
among the main body of the Methodists – and would lead
his little flock out into Rochford market square, there to
harangue them and the crowd together. He couched his
message in homely terms, he had courage, a loud voice, and
a firm belief in himself, all of which he needed to combat
local derision, for his old songs were still remembered and
sung, and it was a new experience to see Jack Banyard
standing on a box conveniently high, and exhorting his fel-
lows to hear the Word of God!

A hostile public response was to be expected, and he did
indeed meet with considerable opposition. Where he
appeared, sticks, stones and brickbats were hurled at him,
while others shouted vulgar abuse, and even took to throwing water over him. A pail of something worse than water
was brought to extinguish him when he appeared in the
main street of Great Wakering, another village nearby, to
preach. The corruption, the worst filth that could be
obtained, was placed before Banyard's face, but the man
who had agreed to throw it lost his nerve when the preacher
blithely continued, and so the contract failed. But the worst
offender in this respect, and one who continually harassed
Banyard, was his old friend and companion of former days,
William Layzell. The story is told how one Sunday evening
when Banyard took up his position in Rochford square,
William Layzell, dressed in a white parson's gown, with his
head uncovered and a book in his hand, came out of a public
house opposite, supported by a comrade, one Canum. They
walked towards Banyard, carrying a chair and a parson's
hat, and when within a yard of the preacher, Canum placed
the chair, and Layzell ascended. He opened his book, and,
matching his delivery to Banyard's, while Banyard preached
to the Brothers, Layzell appealed to the dear Sisters, and
announced he would preach to them for a twelve month and
a day[6].

Banyard's cottage itself came under attack during these
early days: its windows were frequently broken, and sometimes, when services were in progress, songs of praise within
had to compete with shouts of abuse from without. When-
ever the door was opened for worshippers to go in or out,
rotten eggs, and handfuls of mud, earth, and filth gathered

from ditches and the worst places in Rochford, were hurled in by members of the crowd strategically placed, besmearing the walls and the clothes of the Banyardites. Spent missiles of similar materials could be seen adhering to the exterior boards. Sometimes the crowd gathered outside grew so excited that the door had to be bolted, and shutters put up, to prevent worse damage being done. Years later, a Banyardite of a later generation told how he had gone as a boy to hear Banyard preach at a little cottage, again in Great Wakering:

> A little man stood up to preach, and every time the door opened stones and brickbats were hurled in, but they never hit him, and the more they came the more the little man's eyes sparkled and shone[7].

It was counted a sign that God was on their side, that the stones so frequently missed their target.

After about two years in West Street, James Banyard's landlord objected to his preaching in his house any longer, so the Banyardites were compelled to leave these premises, and seek others, which they obtained in Union Lane, Rochford (so called because the Union Workhouse, for the housing of 300 paupers, had been erected here in 1837). This new place was a small house, of which one part was used as a meeting room, and was able to seat about twenty-five, which number the Banyardites did not then muster. To pay the rent of two shillings a week was their greatest difficulty, yet here they formed themselves into a church, with James Banyard their leader, whom they termed Elder. A few church rules were drawn up at the same time, although not then written down, as Banyard would not allow books to be kept. The substance of these was as follows:

> We will have a prayer meeting at five o'clock in the morning before we go to work; and on Tuesday and Thursday evenings at seven. On the Lord's day we will meet at six and half-past ten in the morning; at half-past two in the afternoon; and half-past six in the evening. When we meet to worship the Lord let no vain or worldly thoughts enter your hearts, but keep your minds on the Lord, fall on your knees and ask the Lord to meet with us and bless us.
> At all meetings brothers and sisters may offer their thanks, praises and requests to God the Father and His people, except

Sunday afternoons and evenings, when the leaders will preach
from the Word of God. We will accept no money for preaching,
make no laws, have no book of rules, but the Word of God
alone. For unless one knows his sins are forgiven, and that his
name is in the Lamb's Book of Life, we will not accept him as
a member of the church of God.[8]

Elsewhere it is significantly stated that "Preachers are not to
burden the church, but to subsist by manual labour". All
future practices of the Peculiar People (except healing, of
which more hereafter) are here primitively expressed: the
admittance of new members only after they have experienced
a spiritual 'rebirth'; the total reliance upon, and literal
interpretation of, the Bible; the independence of preachers;
and the Sunday wholly dedicated to worship. Even the times
of meetings and services were to remain unchanged for well
over a hundred years.

The Banyardites continued in Union Lane for about two
years with very little increase, and it proved a hard struggle
to keep the infant church together. One serious division had
already occurred when two of the church members, John
Shepherd and George Bishop, had mistakenly conceived the
notion that religion was all happiness, singing and rejoicing.
When Banyard rejected this error, they left him, and took
half his people with them, even venturing into the open
street to preach against him for several months, until, as the
account happily puts it, they "ultimately melted away as
snow before the sun".

Despite these troubles, Banyard persevered, and in about
1842 managed to obtain better accommodation in an old
tenement in Rochford, called the Barracks near the Marl-
borough Head Inn. In the upper part of this building there
were three rooms. The partition walls were removed, and
a sizeable meeting place resulted, able to hold about one
hundred. Here the work began to revive. Here too began
their practice of divine healing, further manifestations of
which were to make the name of the Peculiar People noto-
rious in days to come. It is easy in the circumstances to
imagine how such a practice could arise. The first instance
of healing among them, however, proves, by the hesitation
of the chief actors, that this was no premeditated act: rather,

that a somewhat frightening power had suddenly and remarkably been revealed to them.

It is said that one of their number, William Perry of Southend, who had lain sick for some years, unable to work, with a consumption, and had tried medical skill but without success, was praying one morning when God spoke to him in the words of James 5:14–15:

> Is any sick among you? Let him call for the elders of the church; and let them pray over him, anointing him with oil in the name of the Lord: And the prayer of faith shall save the sick, and the Lord shall raise him up.

These words were constantly with him until the following Sunday morning, when he determined, if possible, to get to the old Barracks at Rochford, that they might be fulfilled. He convinced two of the brethren to lead him there, whereupon he told James Banyard the words that he had received. Banyard, it is said, was more than a little reluctant to perform the rite, but agreed at last saying, "It is not for me to dampen your faith, brother", and so they got upon their knees. Banyard began to pray, and while thus engaged, "the Lord sent the healing power upon them, which entered William Perry, chasing away all consumption, giving him a perfect deliverance"[9]. As a proof of this, he walked twelve miles that same day, with a brother who was going to preach at an outdoor meeting at Paglesham, and home again; ate a good meal, which he had not done for a long time, and, according to one account, went to work the next day (Monday) in the brickfields at Southchurch near Southend. He lived in good health for many years after.

This phenomenal healing was soon followed and confirmed by others. Charles Porter of Southend, who was suffering from a liver complaint that had not been cured by the doctors, was healed immediately with the laying-on of hands; and so was a Mrs. Gray from the nearby village of Hawkwell, who suffered from asthma. When she felt the cure taking effect, Mrs. Gray is said to have broken out with the words: "Glory be to God: He has healed me". This and other instances were taken to show that God had indeed chosen the Banyardites to be His people, by a special gift of His favour distinguishing them from the unregenerate mass of mankind. "Bless God", said one of the Sisters, "We shall not want any more medicine or doctors!" If God is all-sufficient, and if He had taken them under His wing and made them the apple of His eye, what need was there for them to trust themselves further to the works and skill of men? At least, this is how the Banyardites reasoned, and they were strengthened in their opinion when one of their number, Samuel Hammond, consented to go under an operation and then died, when the surgeon's knife slipped and cut what it was not meant to. They concluded it was far better for them to trust in God rather than in man. And from this followed the doctrine (belief in which was now added to the conditions for membership of the church) of the laying on of hands, and the anointing with oil, and the prayer of faith and the entire abandonment of doctors, their medicine and their skill. The church said that the elders were the most suitable persons for God to heal the sick by, and the sisters in cases of childbirth, it being contrary to the law of nature and of God to solicit the assistance of man in such cases. Needless to say, this doctrine, which to the Banyardites seemed natural and right, to others appeared an abomination, and opposition of a different sort from the flinging of stones and brickbats began to make way against them, at the same time as their name spread far abroad.

In 1848, a great excitement arose in the village of Prittlewell, two miles from Rochford, at the death of a child of a member of the Banyardites. No doctor had been called in to attend the child in its illness, because the father, according to the doctrine he believed in, had had no faith in medical aid, and trusted in God for healing. An inquest followed the death of the child, the first to be held in connection with the death of a Banyardite. Almost everyone in the village and surrounding neighbourhood, it is said, moved against the father of the dead child: bills were stuck about announcing the fact, and a song was composed and sung in the streets, mocking the idea of healing the sick without a doctor. Even the curate of Prittlewell Church joined the foray, by making known his intention, on a selected Sunday, to preach against this so-called delusion. He was an eloquent and learned man, the accounts say, and hundreds from the villages round about came in to hear him. He took as his text, "They that be whole need not a physician, but they that are sick," (Matthew 9:12). Banyard and a number of his followers were among the congregation, but they were not allowed to speak for themselves, and so great was the public demonstration afterwards that some say they were in danger of their lives, and had to be escorted out of the village by the police. Nevertheless, Banyard was determined to go on with his preaching, and immediately announced a Sunday for reply to the curate in defence of the doctrine that he and his followers held so dear. The service was held in the old Barracks at Rochford, which was packed to overflowing. Banyard took the same lesson as the curate and spoke on it, declaring that these words of Jesus in Matthew were clearly intended to be taken in the sense of spiritual healing, and that they in no way contradicted the numerous specific references to physical healing by faith in the Bible. To one of Banyard's followers who was present, Banyard's reply seemed quite conclusively to have "turned the sword into the curate's own bosom". And it would seem as if the curate took that figurative sword very much to heart, for another of our chroniclers adds that "sad to relate, the curate was taken ill, and in a few days expired"[10].

As if to confirm the Banyardites in their course, new cases of divine healing now occurred. A Mrs. Shed, also from nearby Hawkwell, who had lockjaw for three weeks, was able to take food only in a liquid state. At length she wrote on a slate, being unable to talk, that if something was not done, she would certainly die. James Banyard was sent for. He prayed over her, "and in less than five minutes the Lord perfectly healed her". Another case, a cripple from Woodham Ferrers, about ten miles away, who had walked on the side of his foot from birth, was "perfectly healed" when Banyard laid his hands upon him and prayed over him. The foot became straight, he could put the sole of it down onto the ground for the first time, and it would bear his weight. Another man similarly afflicted was Cornelius Ayling, whose backbone was so misshapen that it was visible through his clothing. He had been attended by a doctor in Southend, who had recommended him to the hospital, but instead he had gone to the Banyardites. They accordingly had offered prayers for his recovery, and he was "perfectly healed", the backbone returning to its proper place.

Now the news of these healings began to fly hither and thither, and even reached the pages of the *"Essex Standard"* which, on November 14,1851, accorded the Banyardites an unflattering paragraph:

ENTHUSIASM IN THE NINETEENTH CENTURY

A village in this county, not far from the river Thames, contains a sect of religionists, who lay claim to the power of working miracles. Lately a young cripple was brought into their place of meeting, and desired to throw aside its crutches and walk. The child having cast aside its wooden supporters, immediately fell, but the congregation believed that the infirmity was not removed because the cripple had not sufficient faith. These deluded people refuse all medical aid, even in cases of extreme affliction and suffering.

Doctors and clergymen were alerted to the dangers of this new sect, and some used considerable energy to attempt to wean converts from it. Some farmers went so far as to dismiss known Banyardites from their employ, because of their religion, or to make their work conditional upon their renouncing it, and it was then a hard struggle for the poor labourer to pit his faith against the needs of a wife and family. Young sisters in service were threatened with dismissal by their mistresses, and even in families in these early days, like pressures were sometimes applied, as in the case of one Elizabeth Brown of Canvey Island. Sister Brown's father, it was said, had furnished a cottage for her when she married, but when he heard that she had joined the Banyardites, he was so angry that he removed all the furniture, and she was left with just a few things of her own. She and her husband and two children, reduced by this to utter poverty, were forced to make up their beds with oat husks and such, and to scrape a wretched living. For two years her father refused to speak to her, until one day they met at an auction sale at a neighbouring farm. There, to her astonishment, finding her still resolute, he greeted her by asking if she wanted anything, and then proceeded to purchase for her whatever she required.

The religion of the Banyardites continued to prosper. Banyard's reputation went before him; he had followers in all the villages round about; the healings were much discussed, and there were many friendly houses where they could meet. On Sundays the enthusiastic brethren would set off early to tramp to outdoor meetings further and further afield, often walking twenty miles in all kinds of weather. In this way, the whole of south-east Essex was extensively visited: by today's standards the distances are trifling, but we are writing of a century ago.

> Both rain and hail showered upon them, penetrating their thin clothing, yet they have pursued their way, stood all day and declared the truth, and upon their return in the dark and oft-times bitter cold nights, they have been pleased with a morsel of dry bread to eat as they have journeyed home, where they have arrived sometimes in the morning. Taking off their green smocks, they have attired themselves in their daily apparel, bowing the knees for a short time in prayer, and then partaking of a breakfast which oft-times consisted of bread and a few cold potatoes. They have thus gone forth to their daily toil, full of joy and rejoicing in the God of their salvation[11].

Banyard was helped in this work by men who themselves sometimes had interesting stories to tell: Isaac Anderson, whose life story will be found in an appendix to this book; Samuel Harrod, who had been with Banyard from the very beginning; and Samuel Taylor, an artilleryman stationed at the recently established army garrison at Shoebury. Taylor had deserted his post to attend a meeting of the Banyardites one Sunday evening, was subsequently court-martialled, sent to prison for three months, and then discharged from the Army. After serving his prison term, he returned to Rochford, where James Banyard taught him the shoemaking trade, which enabled him to earn his living. Other converts included John Thorogood of Shoebury, David Handley of Maldon, Samuel Worskett of Woodham Ferrers, and Thomas Rickett of Eastwood.

In 1845, his first wife having died, James Banyard married again; his new bride was twenty-three years his junior, a young widow called Judith Lucking. They moved to a bigger house at 95 North Street, Rochford, and were to have three children, to whom they gave the names Hephzibah, Nehemiah, and Ezra. Judith was the daughter of a local land-owning family, the Knappings, and with money that she kindly advanced, Banyard was able to buy land in Rochford, and build his first chapel, in 1850: this also was in North Street. Here on a Sunday, from 180 to 200 people would assemble from the villages round about – Prittlewell, South-church, Eastwood and Wakering: Banyard would go out to meet them, and enter Rochford singing hymns in procession, with the street crowded behind him. One hymn was a par-ticular favourite:

> The little cloud increaseth still,
> The heavens are big with rain,
> We haste to catch the teeming shower,
> And all its moisture drain.
>
> A rill, a stream, a torrent flows,
> But pour the mighty flood:
> O sweep the nations, shake the earth
> Till all proclaim Thee God.

In the same year, the Banyardites at Prittlewell hired a former Calvinist chapel for worship. As chapels began to be estab-lished, the need for a binding constitution for the church rapidly became apparent, and also for preachers, evangelists and other church officers. And if they were to have chapels, what were they to call themselves? To seek the answers to these problems, they turned, as always when in difficulty, to their Bibles.

In 1852, it was decided to constitute the church, as author-ised in the Bible, with bishops, elders and their assistants, who were to be called helps. There were to be four bishops appointed to overall command: James Banyard, Samuel Har-rod, John Thorogood, and David Handley. To establish this hierarchy, an unique ceremony was held in David Handley's rooms in Maldon. James Banyard was ordained first. The other three laid their hands upon him, and in the name of the Father, and of the Son, and of the Holy Ghost, and by the united desire of the Church, they assigned him their bishop. He now being in power, in turn laid his hands upon them, and the solemn ceremony was repeated.

The next thing to settle was their name. Previously they had been called, among other things, Banyards, Banyardites, Christian Brethren, the Brethren, Newlights, and Ranters[12]. Because they believed that Banyard was undoubtedly the man whom the Lord had chosen to build again His fallen church, because they took instances of divine healing to be a sign of the divine favour, and because they trusted that if they carried out their profession they would indeed be God's own Chosen People, there was one name that seemed to fit their choice, appearing frequently in the Authorised Version of the Bible, in both the Old Testament and the New:

> For thou art an holy people unto the Lord thy God, and the Lord hath chosen thee to be a *peculiar people* unto himself, above all the nations that are upon the earth.
> (Deuteronomy 14:2)
> And the Lord hath avouched thee this day to be his *peculiar people* as he hath promised thee, and that thou shouldest keep all his commandments: And to make thee high above all nations which he hath made, in praise, and in name, in honour . . .
> (Deuteronomy 26:18–19)
> (Jesus Christ) gave himself for us, that he might redeem us from all iniquity, and purify unto himself a *peculiar people* zealous of good works.
> (Titus 2:14)
> But ye are a chosen generation, a royal priesthood, an holy nation, a *peculiar people;* that ye should shew forth the praises of him who hath called you out of darkness into his marvellous light: Which in time past were not a people, but are now the people of God; which had not obtained mercy, but now have obtained mercy.
> (I Peter 2:9,10).

This term was considered very appropriate, and so at the same meeting, after a few consultations, the name of The Peculiar People was decided upon.

Three more chapels of the Peculiar People were built during the year 1852, in very different locations. One was at Woodham Ferrers, and was erected by the enthusiastic Samuel Worksett, of whom mention has already been made; another was at Bath Street in London, built by William Bridges (who had been busily at work all this time proclaiming the gospel in London, and had been down into Essex many times also to preach alongside Banyard)[13]; and the third was on Daws Heath, a hamlet some miles west of Rochford where, in 1853, Bishop Samuel Harrod took up residence. This was a place with a sinister reputation, the inhabitants of which were said to subsist by robberies, so that respectable people feared to cross the Heath after dark. The police would resort to it when anything was lost, and smuggled goods were also believed to pass through here on their way from the coast. It was also the haunt of a white wizard of local fame, one Cunning Murrell, who was probably closely concerned in the smuggling business. When they arrived, the Peculiars very soon straightened the place out; the land was put under cultivation, and many of the worst characters were redeemed and became members of the church. In at least eight other places – Wakering, Foulness Island, Tillingham, Steeple, Maldon, Witham, Herongate and Fobbing, villages widely scattered through Essex – the Peculiar People were certainly meeting in cottages and in small groups by this date, and most of these places were to have their own chapels in time.

In all these ventures Banyard had been prominent: sadly, he now fell into schism with the church he had founded. In 1855, one of his sons was taken very ill, and, the prayer of faith seeming to bring no relief, and fearing that the boy would die, Banyard turned in desperation to a doctor, one whom he had often preached against, and whose physic and practice he had denounced as useless. The doctor was admitted to the house, the child examined, a treatment specified, and a cure ultimately resulted. Not content with this, Banyard now began to preach against his own former opinions, advising the brethren that they too must not hesitate to seek medical assistance in times of illness. The prayer of faith, he declared, was not to be abandoned, but he urged that it might very well be supplemented: faith and medicine working together had raised his son to health, and so it might be with them.

This brought his congregation into a state of division: some contended with Banyard for the doctor, while others were equally determined that he who had led them into the right way, as they saw it, was not going to lead them out of it. After much contention, they concluded that James Banyard, being such a changeable man, should no longer hold the position of their leader. As he owned the chapel at Rochford, it was impossible for them to take it from him, so in a body they rather clamorously withdrew to Prittlewell, and worshipped with the People there instead. Banyard was deposed from his bishopric, and the leadership of the church was transferred to Samuel Harrod, the centre shifting at the same time from Rochford to Daws Heath.

Banyard preached to a depleted following for his few remaining years. He abandoned all his extreme opinions, and to some it must have seemed like a return to much earlier days, with his last congregation no greater than his first, and a doctrine sounding remarkably like traditional Methodism being expounded. In 1863 he fell ill with a diseased foot, but this time medicine failed him, and he died on October 31. His wife wrote in the Cruden's Concordance that bears his signature:

> James Banyard the Beloved Husband of Judith Banyard fell asleep in Jesus half-past two o'clock Saturday Afternoon October 31st 1863. the Friday night my Beloved lifting up His hands exclaimed Glory be to God who can have a better hope than I have got this is the time to prove it. The heavenly smiles on his blessed face was beautiful to behold and said I want this Spirit to depart, lifting up his hands to the last and kissing me with his dear cold lips as long as he could, gave his family into the hands of God. his lips kept moving but no voice. sensible to the last. fell asleep and was buried Friday November the 6th 1863 followed by a large number of people with those that attended the House of God. sung the hymn 'Thee we adore eternal name!' Blessed are the Dead that Die in the Lord [14].

With his death, the first phase of the history of the Peculiar People comes to an end.

CHAPTER II

Expansion and Establishment

James Banyard's successor, Bishop Samuel Harrod had, in 1855, been a member of the Peculiar People for seventeen years. As a boy of eighteen, a labourer in a green smock frock, he had been drawn by Banyard's preaching at the Wesleyan chapel in Rochford, and he had subsequently joined the brethren in the little cottage in West Street, on January 10, 1838. Thereafter he had been active in all the works of the church. He had distinguished himself, when opposition in Rochford was at its height, by venturing out of the cottage one evening to calm a hostile crowd with an impromptu sermon: the congregation within, hearing his success, had thereupon closed their meeting, and come out to join him, a scene which had tended to please James Banyard. It was he who had accompanied William Perry on the afternoon of his deliverance from consumption, and who had preached on this first miraculous healing among the Banyardites, to the villagers of Paglesham. On Daws Heath his labours had transformed "a crime-stained wilderness" into a peaceful agricultural community, and his authority at large was accepted without question. He was a healthy-looking man with red cheeks, below average height but broad and strong, and, like many another countryman, pursued a multiple profession, as thatcher, haybinder, butcher and market gardener. He no longer wore the smock but the countryman's cloth coat and, even when ministering to the brethren, a coloured scarf at his neck.

Harrod began his term of leadership by collecting and compiling, with the assistance of Bishop David Handley and another, the first hymn book of the Peculiar People, which was published at Maldon in Essex in 1860. This collection drew heavily upon a hymn book entitled 'The Stirling', and the Methodist Hymn Book, which had previously been used for their services, but it also included some verses composed by members of the Peculiar People: the lack of such a collection had long been felt[1]. The two Bishops also collaborated in other ways: to carry their religion further, they began surprisingly to preach in various places hired for them in Woolwich, the arsenal town south of the Thames. In 1862 Bishop Handley fell unfortunately into error, and embraced the doctrine of the Christadelphians. He retained his chapel at Maldon, but lost his congregation, which left him and moved a mile or two off, to a small chapel at White Elm under a new leader, Thomas Lloyd, a mill owner.

The work at Woolwich, however, prospered. The house of one George Petchey was opened for preaching, and soon a larger place, a schoolroom in Plumstead, was obtained. A competent and clear-headed young man with energies equal to Harrod's own, Daniel Tansley, led the church, assisted by John Vine, Thomas Hines, George Hurry and Joseph Clarkson, all Woolwich townsmen. When this cause was well established, Tansley and Vine and their wives removed to Canning Town, north of the river, to begin missionary work there in the raw industrial suburbs then springing up. On street corners and in a hired chapel (a former cow shed) in Canning Town they steadily continued, until they were finally able to obtain ground and raise a chapel on Church Street, which was so well attended that it had shortly to be enlarged.

Samuel Harrod, unlike his predecessor, committed to paper and refined the rites and ceremonies of his expanding church. In 1861, tea meetings were instituted to occupy the three public holidays of the year that the labouring poor enjoyed – Good Friday, Easter Monday and Christmas Day. In 1865, Holy Communion was celebrated for the first time at the chapel on Daws Heath, and thereafter throughout the church. In 1867, it having been found that elders going to preach on Sundays sometimes grouped themselves in error at one individual centre to the neglect of others, an Elder's Plan on Methodist lines was drawn up, and the denomination was organised into three 'circuits' or dioceses – London, Witham and Southend – with a bishop at the head of each. In 1870, baptism by sprinkling for converted members only was introduced. New chapels appeared at Tillingham, Herongate, Witham, Stanford-le-Hope, and Ramsden Heath – all villages in Essex.

Meanwhile, the little church at Woolwich, left in the hands of Hurry, Hines and Clarkson, had run into serious trouble. In April 1872, two of Hurry's children died, within a short space, of smallpox, medical aid having been refused, and Hurry was committed to Newgate Prison for trial at the Old Bailey on a charge of manslaughter. Within a few days, another of his children, though removed from the house and inoculated by the doctor, died of the same dread disease. Great alarm and indignation was felt in the neighbourhood, when it was learnt that the ailing children had been brought into crowded meetings to attempt a healing, and that hands had been laid upon them for the same purpose, for by such means a contagious disease could easily be spread. Thomas Hines, one of the elders who had performed this office, was dismissed from his job as coal carter at the Royal Arsenal for refusing to discontinue the healing practice: his plea in his own defence, that he would refrain in future from visiting contagious cases, was rejected by the head of his department. (That official said that 10,000 men working in cramped conditions would be put at risk if he were kept on: also, without a medical opinion, how could Hines distinguish contagious cases?) A few days before the trial, at the inquest on the inoculated child, the coroner expressed his regret at learning that smallpox had increased rapidly in the district, and gave it as his opinion that all the fatal cases could, directly or indirectly, be brought home to the proceedings of the Peculiar People. The trial itself ended inconclusively: the prosecution case broke down when the doctors were asked to state whether the lives of the children could have been saved had medical assistance been sought. No doctor could positively say so: after all, had not inoculation proved ineffectual in the case of the third child? So Hurry was acquitted. Nevertheless, the Grand Jury issued a strongly worded statement, asking for attention to be called to these people who, even in cases of smallpox of a virulent kind, were taking no medical means either to stay the disease or to cure or mitigate the illness of the patient, and who "are in fact practising a doctrine dangerous to the community at large"[2]. They hoped

Left: *Elder Daniel Tansley of Canning Town*

Below: *Sisters Jarvis and Tansley at the graveside of Daniel Tansley*

Above: *Elder Thomas Rayner of Great Wakering (see pp. 38, 51)*

Below: *Original Peculiars' chapel, Daws Heath (see p.27). This is now the home of the author.*

that, if necessary, legislation would be considered and passed to remedy the matter.

Within three years, the Peculiar People at Woolwich were again before the courts. The smallpox scare had subsided: the case now concerned a two-year old child, who had died in his parents' care with chronic inflammation of the lungs, unattended by doctors. Elders Hurry and Hines were again involved, both having anointed the child with oil and prayed over it. The father of the child, John Downs, said that, short of obtaining medical assistance, everything possible had been done. The case was again transferred to the Central Criminal Court, but on this occasion the authorities agreed that Downs should be liberated on condition that the Peculiar People would consent to admit medical aid to such of their children as were in their parents' hands. Hurry and Hines consented. As a result, there were schisms at Woolwich, and at a council meeting of all the elders of the denomination, held at Southend, it was decided that the church should cut them off. The following Sunday, the redoubtable Daniel Tansley went to Woolwich with this pronouncement and, rising amidst opposition in the place, resolved the matter by shouting: "All you who mean to follow in the same old way, and be Peculiars, follow me!:" Whereupon about half the congregation rose and followed him to a brother's house, and remained for some time under Daniel Tansley's care. Hurry, Hines and Clarkson, with the few that remained with them, worked hard to support their more liberal doctrine, but Hines soon grew dissastisfied, and rejoined the church. Hurry and Clarkson then tried to unite with the Salvation Army, failed, and at last started a sect of their own, calling themselves the "Full Salvationists". This also failed, and both ultimately returned to the Peculiar People[3].

The rigid ruling on divine healing and the rejection of doctors among the Peculiar People was maintained. Indeed, in the same year as the troubles at Woolwich, the Peculiars of the London chapel are reported to have hired a large house in Tower Street, Hackney, on the north-east side of London Fields, to put the whole question of the efficacy of unaided faith in healing, to a practical test. A board is said to have been set up before the house, bearing the inscription: "House of Faith, for the reception of such sick as are considered

hopeless incurable, to be healed by the prayer of faith"[4]. This
was supported by the now familiar passages from the Scriptures (Matthew 21:22; James 5:14–16; Mark 16:17–18). Stren-
uous local opposition to this latest venture of Peculiarism
was confidently predicted in the press, but whether the hospital was able to substantiate its claims is not recorded.

Many Londoners of the time concluded, from the publicity
that the churches in Woolwich and elsewhere had received,
that the Peculiar People were a metropolitan sect. Certainly
with the more enterprising country brethren already moving
up into the towns in search of better jobs and higher wages,
the London circuit was kept well supplied, while the work
of the church in Essex was almost unknown outside the
county.

It was in Essex, however, that its main strength lay, and
here the primary centres were all already vigorously branch-
ing. From the chapel at Witham, George Wiles, a baker, had
carried the sect north to Cressing village; and in 1880 a Miss
Tracey, formerly an Anglican (until she heard the Peculiars
preach) opened her cottage in Stanway near Colchester for
meetings of the brethren. A few years later a Brother Barnard
began open air preaching on Totham Plains. Brother John
Hockley came from the group established at Ramsden Heath,
who had themselves originally come from Herongate, to
open a little chapel at South Green. Joshua Hempstead and
Charles Whaley went from Stanford-le-Hope to start a new
branch in Grays. The People who had been at Prittlewell
since 1850 moved into a large place in Southend which, with
the extension of the railway, was rapidly becoming a popular
seaside resort with Londoners – Isaac Anderson was in charge
here, assisted by William Heddle, a young immigrant Scot,
and others. James Banyard's old chapel in Rochford, which
had been closed since shortly after his death, was bought and
reopened, and presided over by one of his original followers,
William Wood.

There were also new places at Great Wakering (leader
Thomas Rayner), at Great Baddow near Chelmsford, and in
the villages of Steeple and Hockley. George Horsnell, a farm
bailiff at The Chase, Thundersley (and a member of Bishop
Harrod's Daws Heath congregation), being sent to manage
a farm at Upchurch in Kent, took his religion with him

there, and started a new cause, though he lost both his home
and his job when he attempted to open his own cottage for
preaching. On Daws Heath itself, membership had so
increased, that in 1880 a new chapel had to be built, with
room for 300 worshippers. Here resided the Bishop of the
Peculiar People with his three assistants – Angelo Chalk,
Henry Anderson, and Frederick Harrod his son[5].

Each new "cause" of the Peculiar People in Essex had a
sturdy local opposition to contend with, and public opinion,
here as in London, remained implacable on the doctrine of
unassisted divine healing, several Peculiars having been committed to the Essex Assizes on charges of manslaughter
(though only one was convicted). Nevertheless, hostility to
the sect had softened in thirty or forty years. Farmers who
had once dismissed brethren from their work force, were
now often found to be employing them in positions of the
highest responsibility (for which their patent honesty and
reliability fitted them) as farm managers and horsemen, and
even defending their good character, if necessary, in the law
courts. Though at the time there was not a single wealthy
man among them, it was generally noted that the brethren
never allowed one of their number to become chargeable to
the poor rate. If a brother was unable to work for his living,
and had no means of subsistence, the church would subscribe
for his support, and maintain him for as long as he remained
in that condition: indeed, it was their boast that no member
of the sect had ever received parish relief of any description.
In ordinary family relations, they were accepted to be well-
nigh irreproachable: the Peculiars were exemplars of sober
good living. Their children were as well educated as conditions would allow, their sick – though they ridiculed the
absurd pretensions of doctors – were lovingly cared for, and
prayers and affection and an abundance of good food lavished
upon them. Alcohol was but sparingly taken (in contrast to
the beer-soaking so prevalent among rural labourers), and
smoking they regarded as an abomination. Their dress was
formal and strange: the men chiefly distinguished in that all
were clean-shaven, save for small side whiskers only; the
women clad in sober Quakerish gowns and black bonnets.
After the labouring week, they met on Sundays to set the
world at naught, in meetings that were loud and fervent and

long, those from a distance taking their food with them, and eating it in chapel in the intervals between services. A great volume of praise issued from these humble meeting places: services were prolonged to a late hour, and the villages which worshippers passed through on their way homewards, were often disturbed by their shouts and singing and clapping of hands.

In 1884, the People's first united Harvest Thanksgiving was held at Chelmsford, the county town of Essex. This was the largest gathering of the sect that had so far taken place, previous thanksgivings at Southend and Daws Heath having proved inaccessible to many in the outlying churches[6]. The increase in numbers had been very marked. In 1855, after Banyard's "fall from grace", the combined congregations of the church had stood at about one hundred Peculiars, according to Bishop Harrod. In 1884, more than thirteen hundred brethren were able to make their way, some with considerable difficulty, to the county town, from the furthest corners of the county. It was no wonder that the proceedings, held in the Chelmsford Corn Exchange, were marked with scenes of the keenest enthusiasm[7].

So successful was this 1884 meeting judged to have been, that another was held the next year in the same place, and the next (though now transferred to the more spacious Congregational Chapel), until it became an annual custom. Each year seemed to bring increase of numbers, and greater enthusiasm.

Bishop Harrod was now sixty-four years old. His whole life had been devoted to work for the church. So commanding was his position that in 1888 a special meeting was held to celebrate not the founding of the sect, but the fiftieth year of his conversion. This Jubilee meeting, as it was called, deferred from the proper date in January until May in hope of better weather, was an overwhelming success, the peak of Harrod's achievement. A large marquee, erected in fields owned by the Bishop in Mill Lane, Rayleigh, a few miles from his chapel, was filled to capacity on the day by 1800 Peculiars. The Bishop sat in the seat of honour on a raised dais, flanked by ten notable elders of the church, with seventeen other deacons seated behind. Elder Daniel Tansley, now Bishop (or Superintendent, as he preferred to call himself) of the London circuit, presided in high good humour, and heaped praises upon his senior.

"When I look at him", he said, "with the health that I have known him to enjoy and the strength he has had, I consider him an exceptional man".

And the congregation responded: "Yes, God bless him".

"I think God has been good to him" ("Yes, yes").

Then presenting the Bishop, on behalf of the church, with a bag of eighty gold sovereigns as a memorial for his services, and an illuminated address, Tansley turned to Harrod and laid his hand upon him, saying quietly: "The Lord bless thee, brother". Aloud he continued: "It is not usual for the younger to lay his hand on the elder, but this is not the usual thing, and I feel I must do it at this time." From the audience came a responsive volley of "Amens." The address, which had been worked in needlework by Sister Anne Blackburn of the London church, read:

> Glory to God in the highest. 1838–1888. A token of love and respect, Presented to Samuel Harrod of Thundersley, late of Rochford, In honour of His Jubilee and Fifty Years Faithful Services amongst the Peculiar People. He was converted to God, 1838; went forth to preach, 1838; made a Bishop, 1852. The givers of this small token trust that the recipient will long be spared to continue his Master's work amongst His people and that, when he is called to the Home above, This will fall into the hands of those who will preserve it In honour of the much loved Friends and Brother Samuel Harrod, Bishop of the Peculiar People, The twenty-first day of May, eighteen hundred and eighty-eight[8].

An even more flattering testimonial of his popularity was the set of verses composed especially for the occasion.

> Hail! Brother Harrod, we're glad to see
> The Lord has been so good to thee.
> 'Midst conflict sharp and weighty cares,
> He's kept thee faithful fifty years.
>
> Upheld by God's Almighty hand,
> Firm and unmoved in trust you stand.
> Though levell'd at from earth and hell,
> Still fifty years you have stood well.
>
> With armour on you've kept the field,

The Lord has been your strength and shield.
The Gospel trump you've sounded sweet
These fifty years, and no retreat.

What wonders by thee God hath wrought;
From death to life souls have been brought,
Many released from bonds and fears,
By preaching Christ these fifty years.

Much has been done to mar thy fame,
Reproaches heaped upon thy name,
Still this one truth thy spirit cheers,
God has sustained thee fifty years.

And like a pillar now,
You neither crouch nor bend nor bow,
The sovereign line 'twixt wheat and tares
You have proclaimed these fifty years.

Great God! thine honoured servant spare
Yet many years to labour here;
Till beckoned from his sweet employ
To mansions of eternal joy.

The People thoroughly enjoyed themselves. Elder Thomas
Rayner of Great Wakering delighted them with memories of
the early days and their progress since then. He thanked God
that a better day had dawned for them, in succession to the
scant table and the smock frock. He said he remembered
their noble Bishop wearing the smock, and why? To hide
his poor rags, keep the wind off and make him warm: he
knew what smocks were for, because he had worn one
himself. He remembered singing, 'A better day is coming',
but now he thought they should sing, 'A better day has
come'! (Loud shouts of "Yes, praise the Lord!"). Harrod in
his turn reflected on what the People had learned in fifty
years, by revelation and by suffering. They had gained in
experience as they had come along, he said, and he thanked
God that they were not stupids now. ("No, no!").

It was left to Daniel Tansley, at the evening meeting, to
look into the future. He remembered that in his experience
when there was a question, "What shall we do?" the decision
has been, "Stand our ground, and God will protect us". And
God had, and they were going up, up, up! (Shouts of "Bless

the Lord, we are."). People had said that they were like
mushrooms; they had sprung up but would soon go down,
but such people forgot, he said, that the Lord was on their
side, and that they were on the mount ("Praise the Lord; we
are, too!"). "What shall we be in another fifty years time?"
said Brother Tansley. "I cannot tell. Fifty years hence if this
church shall expand according to the number now before us,
bless the Lord the county of Essex will be warm with us!"
(Laughter, and shouts of "Yes, we hope so!")[9]. And with
this thought, and a hymn, and a blessing, the meeting closed.

In fifty years great changes had indeed been wrought, in
the church and in the lives of the labouring People. The
railways had come to the countryside; trains now rhythmi-
cally marked their passage through a landscape that James
Banyard and his brethren had seen as uninterrupted field and
wood. In the stackyard after harvest, 'the snort and clatter of
the portable steam engine and barnwork had largely replaced
the threshing with hand flails: Elder Thomas Lloyd of White
Elm was one of the local threshing contractors who hired
out the equipment. Steam ploughs worked the land on many
farms in spring; and the single-horse reaper was ending the
long supremacy of the man with the scythe in the harvest
field. To the west, London had spilled over onto the Essex
marshes: new factories poured thick, noxious smoke and
fumes over the suburbs (lately overwhelmed villages) of
West Ham, Plaistow and Barking, the area which Daniel
Tansley had taken as his province. Escaping suburban excur-
sionists were beginning to appear in fancy travelling wear in
country lanes, and artisans were coming out to look for
villas in the rural backwater.

In 1875, the English corn market, unprotected since the
repeal of the Corn Laws, collapsed in one disastrous year,
when grain from the newly-opened prairies of Canada and
the United States flooded the English market. The price of
wheat dropped dramatically; wheat farmers all over the eastern counties went bankrupt, and hundred of labourers were
put out of work. In succeeding seasons, the pressure of
foreign competition was maintained: rents fell, the tenant
farmers of Essex – which of all eastern England was most
seriously affected – worked themselves half to death, trying
to make the heavy clay lands profitable, and the exodus of

the rural population, mainly to London, continued at an alarming rate. Country ploughmen and labourers who had scarcely looked beyond their villages before, were driven to work in factories in Barking and Poplar, in the sugar refineries on Silvertown Wharf, in the Gas Works on Beckton marshes, or to navvy in the recently expanded dockyards. (Successful missions were established in all these places from Canning Town in the 1880s, to draw up the brethren emigrating from the countryside). Now cottages and even farms stood idle and empty, and land dropped out of cultivation on all sides, growing only crops of thistles or turned to rank pasture; the fields, planted with wheat or beans, producing more weeds than corn. While a government dominated by industrialists and liberal reformers looked on impassive and even applauding, the antiquated and obsolescent rural society shook itself to pieces. Addressing his own flock at Harvest Thanksgiving in the year following the Jubilee, Bishop Harrod, himself a small land-owner and market gardener, spoke with understandable bitterness:

> Some of you who have land under your own cultivation know very well how our great men, the legislators, Government people, have treated the land in these last few years by letting it go to rack and ruin. Anyone who has got any judgement of the country and agricultural things may see plainly that our country is falling, and fast too, for one reason: they are letting the land, or a great deal of it, lie uncultivated, and it's going to rack and ruin, which certainly must be the support of our Government properly speaking, and if that goes other things must go in time. It may take time to do it, but it certainly will. Tenant farmers have had to break (been made bankrupt) by tithes, parish charges and rents. Next it must go to the landlords, and then when the landlords go, where must it come to then? It's evident that's the state of the country; but in the midst of the grumbling, I feel we have cause to be thankful to God ("Praise Him"; "Yes"). I believe God has sent as much as the country deserves. I mean in this way. If we don't do our duty to the land, how can we expect great profits? ("No, no"). Can God give increase to that which is not sown or not done? That is our part just as it is to find salvation. Man must make a start and then God will meet him ("Bless Him"). There's crops of only two quarters to the acre all parishes through. But if you don't grow crops don't expect God to send increase. 'Tain't in noways reasonable. A shortened crop is on the land's side and

not on the Lord's side. I am endeavouring to clear Him –
leastways the Lord is clear without me – but I'll speak a word
for Him ('Yes, yes')"[10].

By 1889 the crisis had reached its height. In the following
years many arable farms were recovered for grazing, and
during the First World War much cultivation of necessity
returned. But fifty years of change that had included the ruin
of the agricultural system were obviously not altogether to
the advantage of a church bound so closely to agricultural
ways, and it was clear that, however the Peculiar People
evolved in years to come, they would themselves be
changed, and have to respond to new circumstances.

Bishop Harrod was not to be on hand to lead them into
the twentieth century. Regrettably, only too soon after the
remarkable meeting to celebrate his fifty years' membership
of the church, an even more remarkable schism took place.
Ugly rumours began to fly and attach themselves to the
name of the grand old man of Peculiarism. His private
behaviour was brought into question – no point of doctrine
was involved. Words of scandal linked the name of this
genial, seventy-years-old family man with that of a married
woman of his flock. The facts of the case are obscure, but
it seems that Harrod's resignation was called for, which he
apparently refused to give. The charge was serious enough
for a meeting of elders to be convened at Forest Gate in
November 1890. Harrod was present, but broke it up with
the words: "I shan't say any more. Do with me what you
like, or rather what you can." Again in January 1891 at
Southend he was heard at length, but failed to explain himself. He abruptly ended this discussion by calling out: "I
shall go and take my place, and those who like can come to
me", whereupon he left with two of the brethren. This being
considered an act of withdrawal, the elders further consulted,
Harrod being absent, and decided to separate him from
them, and deprive him of his bishopric. A letter was sent to
the brethren at Daws Heath:

> From the Elders of the Peculiar People to the Church at Daws
> Heath.
> Dear Brethren, We are requested and authorised by all the
> brethren who attended a special council meeting on the 23rd
> day of February 1891, to inform you that Bro. Samuel Harrod's

bad conduct forbids us to hold any further fellowship with him under the present circumstances, and our advice is that he leave the desk, as we cannot recognise him as a preacher and teacher, among us the Peculiar People . . . ."[11]

When a body of elders visited the church the following Sunday, however, they found it locked against them. Harrod was angry that he had not been invited to attend the council meeting that had sealed his fate, and besides, as he paid the rent for the chapel, he believed he could do with it as he liked. The visiting elders held their service in consequence on the chapel forecourt, where, unfortunately, Tansley delivered himself of the opinion that "they had been deceived by a bad man for years." It was upon remarks such as these that Harrod's followers grounded their belief that Tansley was responsible for the whole business: it was all his fault, they said; he was ambitious, and coveted the Bishopric for himself. Two angry factions had sprung up.

The next Sunday, when the chapel was opened again, and Harrod entered to preach, he found that most of his congregation, including his own son and daughter, had deserted him, and gone to meet in a hired room over a shop in Rayleigh. Only about fifty had remained faithful to him. It was a melancholy end to a lifetime of effort. In about a twelvemonth, he handed the key of the chapel back to the landlord, and the congregation returned from Rayleigh under new leaders. Bishop Harrod himself erected another chapel for his own followers, about half a mile along the Heath, which opened in 1894.

Daniel Tansley did indeed become head of the main church, which retained its name, though its members henceforth were more generally known as "Tansleyites". Harrod's people opened new chapels – in addition to the one on Daws Heath – at Southend, Tillingham, Cressing, Hockley, Steeple and Rochford, all within Harrod's circuit, and often close by those of the opposite party. They called themselves the "Original Peculiar People", which name they chose because, they said, they had got the original Bishop.

Within ten years, both leaders were dead, Tansley in 1897 and Harrod in 1898. Paul Spicer of Hockley then led the "Harrodites", and William Heddle of Southend, a credit draper in a thriving business, the Tansleyites. And these new leaders had not been elected two years before the church was broken by another division. In 1900 the Liberty Section of the Peculiar People arose out of the ranks of the Heddleites, demonstrating by copious scriptural references that in their opinion the church had been wrong to undertake that the doctrine of divine healing should be made binding upon its members. They concurred with public opinion that the refusal to accept medical aid was a wrong-headed option, without biblical warrant. They printed an "Article" setting out their beliefs, in which they undermined the significance of the principle, and they concluded:

> We believe that in times of sickness it is the will of God, for us to seek His aid in the way He has appointed in His Word, viz: By the laying on of hands, and by the anointing with oil, and by prayer and fasting, looking to Him for deliverance and healing, if it is in accordance with His divine will.
>
> But observation has shown us that God is not disposed to heal *immediately* in all cases, consequently we consider there is a necessity to know how to deal with sickness and disease.
>
> Moreover, we consider that those who conscientiously feel that they ought to obey the law (in having medical advice for their children), should have the LIBERTY OF THEIR OWN JUDGEMENT in the matter.
>
> And we agree that the whole tenor and scope of both the old and new testament scriptures, do not warrant nor justify the making the doctrine of divine healing a bond of Christian fellowship[12].

When this affirmation was rejected by the Heddleites, the churches of Poplar, Totham, Stanway, Woolwich, Grays and London broke away to form their own union of Libertyites, refusing to accept the ruling of the Heddleites, and appointed as their own Bishop, Joshua Hempstead of Grays. Among the Elders who took their churches with them into the Liberty Section, was George Hurry of Woolwich, veteran martyr to the cause at Woolwich twenty-five years before.

Thus the Peculiar People entered the twentieth century.

CHAPTER III

Change

Elder James Chignell of Witham, speaking at a Harvest Thanksgiving held at Chelmsford in 1901, noted in passing how few of the brethren of the Peculiar People now contributed to the gathering in of the harvest, whereas some six or seven and thirty years before, when he had first joined the movement, "we were most all harvestmen". What changes his generation had lived through! He remembered how at one time of day the men had depended on the harvest bonus to pay their rents and keep out of the Union: how they had struggled on from week to week – working hard all day, and making and mending shoes, some of them, a great part of the night – to buy the necessities for daily existence, bread and flour and coals. Some, he knew, had not tasted meat from one weekend to the next. True, they generally had a large loaf, but sometimes it was "ropey": when you pulled the crumbly pieces apart, the bread stretched like cobwebs, and that had to last all week. Sugar – as black almost as treacle – was fivepence a pound, and tea four shillings a pound. His wages at that time were 12s a week, and out of that it had cost him 7s for bread and flour, and 2s for rent, so there was not much left for extras after that. Said Brother Chignell: "I have worked very hard for a little man, and too hard, but thank God, that time is over, and I am pleased that I have Brothers and Sisters with me not in that position"[1].

The younger, lettered generation indeed considered themselves well out of it. Those who were harvestmen still, blessed the easier times, improved wages and conditions; and those who had gone into the towns had reason to be grateful also. For, as Elder James Southgate, speaking on behalf of the Canning Town church, told the same meeting:

If we have not been favoured to meet in the harvest field to
labour and to toil, we have been blessed with more rest and
time to pray for those that have. That has been our object and
our prayer day and night – that God would bless our Brethren
in the country who were toiling and gathering in the precious
grain . . . I thank the Lord today for the fruits. I might express
my feelings of which I have tasted of. Some beautiful plums
and apples, and various fruits ("*Grapes!*") – yes, and grapes that
God has bestowed upon us . . . I have not got one plum tree
in my garden, nor yet an apple tree (A voice: "*I have, praise the
Lord!*"), but they come round to my door and God has blessed
me with money that I can buy a pennyworth, and they are very
cheap today – plums a penny a pound. Who would be without
jam for the winter? ("*Yes, who?*")We have got some potted
down. I bless the Lord for some small things which you country
people, who live amongst them, would perhaps hardly look at.
There's the blackberries, the last fruit, I think. My wife put
down apple and blackberry – a very nice jam, that. ("Praise the
Lord!") We have got something for praying, have we not? and
we will still keep praying . . .²

As another brother put it, they had got out of Grumbling
Lane and into Thankful Street.

The new Bishop of the denomination, William Heddle of
Southend, had been a member of the Peculiar People since
1873. In earlier days, Elder Heddle tramping the Essex roads
with parcels of merchandise strapped to his chest and back
– he was in the credit drapery business – had been a familiar
sight to many of the brethren working in the fields, who
had benefited from his trade. He too had prospered in the
changing times. A small man with a clear business head, he
was also a fervent and active preacher, and noted for his
charity to the poorer brethren.

Under Bishop Heddle, the elaboration of church ritual
continued. The untidy arrangements for the administration
of Holy Communion were replaced by a regular celebration
at three-monthly intervals throughout the churches. A com-
prehensive revision of the hymn book was undertaken. The
Marriage Service, the Burial Service, the procedure for the
ordination of Bishops, Elders and Helps, were also revised.
Elders or Helps who presumed to transfer from one church
to another without sanction of the Council learned to feel
the full weight of its displeasure. Recommendations ranging

from a disapproval of the reading of indelicate scriptures in public, to a condemnation of the conducting of a milk business on Sundays, flowed from newly created committees.

More substantial matters were also discussed and changes made. A fund was agreed to keep the aged poor out of the workhouse, some of whom, it was learned in 1903, had recently died there in unpleasant circumstances: the gathering of monies for such a purpose was admitted as a charity to relieve a present need. Organised provision for the sick and unemployed was also suggested at the same time: on this, however, opinion was thoroughly divided. It was considered by some that for them to form a sick benefit "club" as suggested, made up of contributions from each supporter to provide against his own possible future troubles, would do nothing less than subvert the will of God: it was far from demonstrating a proper faith. (In the same way, brethren insuring the lives of themselves or their children were not approved.) William Heddle himself led the attack. In 1910, he told a Council of gathered elders:

> The direction of the Lord to his sick is to call for the elders etc. etc. Seek the Lord for healing and to examination and humility and confessing of faults, one to another, and pray for one another that they may be healed, and if we, "God's people", provide a club for sickness, I for one firmly believe we shall have sickness. "For our God is a jealous God."[3]

His rejection of the sick "club" idea was supported by a long list of biblical examples individually examined (e.g. "Proverbs 6:6 & 8: 'Go to the ant thou sluggard and be wise: she provideth in the summer and gathereth in the harvest': personal diligence is taught: no 'club' taught whatsoever"), which proved unanswerable. Still, the need remained and a fund was required, so a compromise scheme was soon forthcoming: instead of fixed contributions, voluntary offerings placed in boxes designated for the relief of the sick and poor, were to be gathered from each church, and redistributed according to need: in this way, the same money would be made available, but transmuted into a charity, a preferable form. When in the following year, Lloyd George, then Liberal Chancellor, introduced his National Insurance Act (1911), which made a sophisticated type of the "club" system mandatory, the Peculiar People were able to negotiate to maintain their own insurance scheme by forming themselves into an Approved Society under the Act, which allowed them to operate independently within the national law[4].

Here they were already on quaking ground, and other social reforms of the time were even harder to accept. The Children's Act of 1908, for example, unwisely connoted a failure to call in medical aid to a sick child, with criminal neglect, and so made conviction in these cases almost inevitable, and harsher sentencing the norm. The Peculiar People set up a special fund to aid such convicted brethren, and stood by their religious commitment in the matter. The Midwives Act (1902), made it illegal for a woman to practise as a midwife after 1st April 1910, without medical certification. This was intended to deal with untrained women who imposed upon the public, but it also affected the much-respected Peculiar midwives, who occupied a very special place in the cares and affections of the Peculiar People, because of their unique responsibility, doctors being as rigorously excluded from scenes of childbirth as from the chambers of the sick and dying. As the Peculiar midwives would never submit to undergo medical training, and as the church did not consider the issue large enough to contest, Sisters in future were advised to be attended by certified midwives from outside the church, only ". . . sisters in the Church to be with them, if possible"[5], which was tantamount to saying that their skills were superseded. In another instance, the intrusive power of the State to enter a home and remove a sick child for treatment, provoked the barren recommendation of the Peculiars' Council: "That in the case of being compelled to have our Children medically treated . . . that they be treated at home rather than taken away to Hospital or Infirmary"[6], where faith in God is perforce reduced to a kind of obstinacy.

Meanwhile, despite division, new missions continued to be planted. In Kent, Walter Horsnell extended the work from Upchurch to Gillingham (New Brompton); in west Essex, Brother Frank Norman, a potato salesman, opened a storehouse at the back of his property at Chadwell Heath near Romford, for worship; to the north, Brother George Smith hired a ramshackle old cottage for the same purpose at Wakes Colne, on the borders of Suffolk. Missionary work from Southend led to the erection of an iron structure for meetings at Wickford in mid-Essex; and a successful group was also formed at Leigh-on-Sea. New chapels were also built at Rochford and Cressing, to replace those lost to the Originals in these villages in 1891. Finally, a Trust Deed, enrolled in Chancery in 1906, ensured that however ruinous might be future divisions, properties of the Church at least would be held in common for the benefit of all; that no factious Bishop or Elder could in future claim or close a chapel at will. This document also contained the first clear account of church doctrines, and the constitution of the church government. The evidence was that the Peculiar People were still increasing.

In 1911 and 1912, also, positive steps were again taken to end the division with the Originals, who had not experienced a like expansion. When Paul Spicer, their nominal leader, obscurely resolved to maintain his independence, and opened a fresh place at Prittlewell[7], a schism in the ranks of the Originals was precipitated, and a party for reconciliation sprang up, headed by George Harrod of Southend, a nephew of the late Bishop. Joseph Nunn, the aged leader of the Originals in the village of Steeple, falling ill at about this time (the leader of the Originals at Tillingham, William Bridge, had died in the previous year), George Harrod took the reunion proposals to his bedside, and asked him: "What shall we do? Shall we go on with it?", receiving the heartening reply: "George, go on with it: do what you can for peace". Joseph Nunn died, and negotiations were opened with Bishop Heddle.

At their first meeting, Bishop Heddle and Elder Chignell, as representatives of the main body, confronted their opposites in the Original party, George Harrod and James Anderson (Rochford) with the Scriptures, and a copy of the Deed Poll for reference, determined that if any doctrinal difference should be raised, they would wish them good day and depart. To their joy, the eleven tenets and three practices described in the Deed Poll[8] were accepted without argument – "our Brethren didn't attempt to pull it about nor raise any discussion" said Bishop Heddle with satisfaction – so that they were soon able to confine their talk to minor personal differences, which, it was agreed, could easily be resolved.

Bishop William Heddle of Southend

The Thanksgiving.

The Thanksgiving Meeting at Southend
Was held, I'm glad we did attend,
To meet with those we love, and join
In work so pleasant, so divine.

As usual, it began with Song,
A proper one, and not too long;
The Twenty-second was the one,
And it was in the Spirit sung.

Our Worthy Bishop, he was there,
And he did next engage in prayer;
Which like sweet Incense did arise
To Israel's God beyond the Skies.

Again we sang a Hymn of praise,
And thus we all our hearts did raise;
To Him whose mercy and whose grace
Had brought us thus before His face.

And so the speaking it began,
And Brother Butcher was the one
Who first arose to praise the Lord;
For ever be His name adored.

He spoke of places where he'd been,
Of worldly mirth, but ne'er had seen
Such cheerful faces as he then
Beheld before him at Southend.

He spoke of God's great power to save,
Who snatched him from a drunkard's grave;
And raised him from the depths of sin,
That he might life immortal win.

Old Brother Wiles, from London, too
Said, " I must praise the Lord with you,"
" To me, indeed He has been kind,
And to adore him I'm inclined."

Our Bishop spoke too, in his turn,
And when he speaks we always learn
Something that's good, if only we
Are wise, and walk obediently.

He spoke of God's great love and power,
Which we all prove each passing hour;
And bade us always faithful prove.
To Him who merits all our love.

September 26th, 1881.

"The Thanksgiving", by Brother James Cooper of Witham, 1881

So, instead of wishing each other good day, they ordered tea and spent the evening together. The irrelevance of twenty years of schism could not have been more aptly demonstrated.

It was the same when the various Original churches seeking reunion – Tillingham, Steeple, Daws Heath, Rochford and Southend – were separately consulted, Bishop Heddle and a small committee making the journeys to the further chapels in Elder Moss of Rayleigh's new motor-car. Wherever the two parties met, a spirit of forgiveness and almost complete unanimity prevailed: within the year, reunion was officially declared amid general rejoicing.

A grand reunion meeting was arranged to celebrate the event at Southend on New Year's Day 1913. Peculiars flocked to the meetings, for the afternoon, and particularly for the evening service. The hall hired for the purpose proved too small to accommodate all, so many brethren not having been expected, and considerable crowding was experienced: however, it was considered by a number of those present that division of the company for an overflow meeting would be undesirable in the circumstances.

The evening meeting created a record in attendance. The hall was crowded to suffocation as the meeting commenced: the doorways themselves were filled, even the adjoining tea-room had its complement of listeners. As the preachers began, the great audience came alive with spontaneous exclamations and rounds of clapping and stamping. The hymns especially were taken up in the characteristic Peculiar fashion, some half dozen verses being extended to a quarter of an hour of the wildest rapture, the women in their excitement throwing their hands into the air in time to the music.

As the evening proceeded, the enthusiasm increased until it had reached a great height. About eight o'clock it broke out in a quite remarkable manner. Brother Horsnell, who hails from New Brompton, was in the middle of an impassioned harangue of congratulation at the happy events which had led up to the meeting, when words failed him to express his thoughts. He jumped up and down several times, shouted out "Praise the Lord" and, waving his arms in the air, turned and faced Bishop Heddle, who spontaneously stood up from his chair. Instantly the two clasped each other round the neck, and kissed each other, almost falling over as they did so. The excitement was

infectious, and at once the whole audience rose up with waving
hands, and, amid ejaculations of "Praise be to God" and "Hallelujah", somebody started a hymn and everybody commenced
to sing with thundering emphasis "Glory – honour – praise –
and – power". The scene was extraordinary. Many of the men
shook hands to the rhythm of the music, others roared at the
top of their voices, and shut their eyes in the ecstacy of the
moment. From the back of the platform came a measured thud-
ding as half-a-dozen people stamped out the time . . . "Glory
– honour – praise – and power" chanted the audience again and
again to the tramp, tramp of hundreds of feet, until it seemed
as though they would go on for an hour. It was quite ten
minutes of almost delirious excitement before the emotion of
the moment passed and the speaker was able to resume his
address[9].

One old brother who left the meeting at about this time to
get a breath of fresh air, died in the street a few minutes
later, presumably of heart failure. This was George Thorington of Daws Heath, aged 76, who had been one of Bishop
Harrod's first converts on the Heath more than sixty years
before. For the past few months, though in poor health, he
had thought of nothing but the reunion. On the day previous
to his death, he is said to have told a friend: "I have a strong
desire to go to the meeting at Southend tomorrow, because
I have counted on them a good deal. If I can only see the
People at the re-union meetings, I don't care if the Lord
takes me the same day!"[10] He spent his last day on earth, as
he would have wished, on his feet, praising and singing with
the reunited brethren.

A year and a half later, these joys already seemed far away.
The Original chapels at Southend and Steeple had been added
to the preachers' Plan; the redundant places, at Tillingham
– where the rival chapels had opposed each other across the
main street – and at Rochford, had been tactfully disposed
of[11]. A Church Building fund had been started, and an evangelical magazine called "*Rays of Light*" had begun to appear
monthly from printing presses in Southend. Determined
efforts had been made, albeit unsuccessfully, to win back the
still-thriving Liberty Section into the Church. Then in September 1914, war was declared, and the church plunged at
once into more conflict, and even deeper divisions than
before.

In 1914, the annual Harvest Thanksgiving at Chelmsford
had to be abandoned – the government having comman-
deered the Corn Exchange and all other large buildings in
the county town – so a big meeting was held at Southend
instead a fortnight later. There, sadness at current troubles
in the world – Bishop Heddle described it as the usurpation
of Satan in the enlightened nations – mingled strangely with
the keen annual analysis of crops, and general rejoicing. The
war was still a long way off. Elder Thomas Rayner of Wakering was even optimistic about it:

> So far as we are concerned as a nation . . . it could not have
> come at a better time; it has come when our harvest is just
> gathered in, when we have got our wheat, our corn in our own
> country, and we hope by the time that our crops may be
> exhausted, there will be a great turn of the tide . . . If it had
> come in May or June, how much worse it would have been![12]

In fact, the church was quite unprepared for any such emer-
gency. When the constitution had been framed for the Deed
Poll of 1906, the possibility of war had not even been discussed, so that no distinct ruling on a Christian's duty in
such circumstances could be found there. The Council of
Elders, conscious of differences in its own ranks, failed even
to issue a statement in the crisis. War fever entered the breasts
of many of the young Peculiars, and off they went, church-
men all, and very few of them ever came back.

Worse was to follow. As 1915 advanced, it was clear that
the government was contemplating introducing conscrip-
tion. In January 1916, indeed, the enabling legislation, contained in the Military Service Act, came before Parliament
for approval. The War and its confusions suddenly moved
closer to home: the question of a Christian's duty could no
longer be evaded. A special Council of the Peculiar People
therefore met, and a long and divided discussion took place,
culminating at length in the following characteristic
statement:

> That the Council of the Peculiar People believe and maintain
> that War and Bloodshed is the work of Satan and absolutely
> contrary to the principles of the religion of Our Lord and
> Saviour Jesus Christ and the teachings of the New Testament.
> We believe that Human Life is sacred and that we may not and
> cannot take human life nor engage in any work that requires

taking the Military Oath. Nevertheless we leave such decision open to the Judgement of every individual whether they will sacrifice their own lives or submit to inflict death upon others (Amendment 1289A – "Yet we do not consider our unity should in any way be affected thereby"). – Our Council will support our Brethren when they conscientiously refuse Military Service, And will assist them in trying to gain exemption therefrom[13].

Conscientious objectors were advised to seek work of national importance (other than munitions), such as in agriculture or market gardening, for the duration: in the event of their failing to obtain this, one body of opinion arose in the church advocating that conscripts should consent to non-combatant service in the forces (principally with the Royal Army Medical Corps), even though this would require taking the Military Oath. It was argued that such work was entirely humanitarian, and would not conflict with Christian principles, as there would be no direct involvement in the fighting: also, it was a Christian's duty to obey as far as possible, the laws of the country in which he dwelt (I Timothy 2:1–6; Romans 13:1–10 etc). The argument on the other side was that even joining the Army to tend the wounded was a participation in an ungodly conflict, and a contribution to the work of Antichrist.

Here was a delicate matter. In May, with the Act about to receive the Royal Assent, the Council, still moving cautiously to avoid a schism, exercised its judgement in the matter, as follows:

As we cannot form another's conscience nor direct their actions, We agree to maintain Christian fellowship with them whichever course their conscience may lead them to take with regard to the Military Service Act. Those who cannot accept Military service shall have our prayers and support, And those who do submit to Non-combatant service, have our prayers (and support)[14]

The words in parentheses were added in an amendment, and approved by "a less majority". This allowed the young men of the church to apply for non-combatant service if they so desired. Some did; some indeed were able to obtain "work of national importance". But inevitably, there remained those who would not compromise themselves in any way with the military authorities. These were the true conscientious objectors who refused to serve in any capacity, and who suffered for their convictions, terms of imprisonment with hard labour at Dartmoor and Wakefield Jails between 1916 and 1918.

Brother Ernest Hockley of Barking was one of these. A Sunday School teacher with the Peculiar People for ten years, he stood by his firm deep-rooted conviction that "war is contrary to the teachings of Jesus Christ", resisting all attempts at persuasion to the contrary, and was sentenced to six months' hard labour (commuted to 112 days), to be served at Dartmoor, in the summer of 1916. There he joined about a score of the brethren currently serving similar sentences, with 1,200 other conscientious objectors – representatives of some 25 to 30 denominations, along with some Socialists and Communists. All wore "broad arrows", the convict's uniform.

For Hockley, hard labour took the form of repairing mail-bags that other prisoners had sewn incorrectly: a heap of them would be thrown into his cell each day. He recalls how beautifully those mail-bags were made, meticulously stitched, with corners "mitred" together (he uses the carpenter's term, for that was his profession). Some others of the brethren were set to making ships' fenders out of thick ropes, and others again were employed in the cookhouse, where at least they were able to pick up the odd scraps. The food was consistently bad, it was almost the worse part of the ordeal, and there was very little of it: 1 pint of skilly and 2 or 4 ounces of bread for breakfast at 7 o'clock, and the same again at 4 o'clock in the afternoon, with a midday meal that varied from day to day (this was called "A" Diet). Some men even managed to put on weight with this wretched food, but their faces were bloated, and none looked healthy upon it. Meals were taken in the main hall of cells, with prisoners sitting at tables of eight, and one man was delegated to read out notices for the day (One day, Hockley received an announcement to read out detailing the activities of the SSS – the "Sanctified Sons of the Saviour". He was later disturbed to discover that the initials in fact stood for the Socialist Sunday School, a persuasion which he could not have been expected to have looked upon with favour). Exercise was limited to two quarter-hour sessions "on the

ring" each day, in a courtyard 50-75 feet across, with high
walls on all sides. Any man caught talking as they walked
round and round a yard apart, was given three days on bread
and water. The same punishment was meted out to any man
caught looking out of his cell window during the day. The
one relief for the men with religious convictions was the
weekly praise meeting with prayers, and the occasional open
air meetings that the authorities allowed[15].

At home, in unprecedented circumstances, the People continued to live and worship as far as possible according to the
ideal that William Heddle had placed before them in 1916,
that they should say: "I have been saved and am not of the
world, and want nothing to do with it". Consequently,
military matters were not discussed in public services, and
elders in khaki (they were very few) were advised to remain
out of the desk for the duration. However, with war on
every friend and stranger's lips, with the ever-present danger
of aeroplane and Zeppelin attacks concentrated on the east
coast within range of Germany, with the scarcity of labour
on the farms, and the mind-numbing casualty lists in the
newspapers, these were only an artificial restraint. The fact
of war, and the disillusion of war, entered all their lives. It
was not a happy time for religious proselytizers.

After the War and its troubles, the chances of a revival for
the brethren began to look more and more unlikely.
Troubles now came upon the church apace. In 1918, the
potent threat of a new faith, in the shape of the Pentecostal
movement, arrived from America, with youth and vigour
on its side, and swept the country, proclaiming the gift of
"tongues" as the Peculiars had once proclaimed the gift of
healing. The Council of Elders moved with unwonted speed
against this sudden threat and its attractive force, condemn-
ing the speaking in tongues as "a sign of spiritual infancy",
and stating their conviction that the "baptism of tongues is
not essential for spiritual perfection (I Corinthians 14th
Chapter)"[16]. Nevertheless, many brethren, dissatisfied with
their own church, experimented with the new faith, and
undesirable manifestations of Pentecostalism even began to
appear in Peculiar services, which being opposed, defections
to the rival movement grew.

The Liberty Section of the Peculiar People was equally

affected. With a new urgency, attempts were renewed to return them to the church, the opening proposals coming, as before, from the breakaway section. Elders Herbert Goobey of Poplar, and Edward Brazier of Totham, Libertyites, took the initiative as the result of a conversation in the Blackwall Tunnel in London in 1920, where they walked till nearly midnight, discussing the spiritual condition of the church and their desire for total reconciliation; parting at last with tears in their eyes, and something rising in their throats, and the affirmation: "Whatever happens, we must be Peculiars to the end of the chapter". Their urgency communicated itself to all six Liberty churches, and a general move towards reunion began, following the pattern of the Originals' seven years before. But this time there was little internal disruption, hardly even an opposing voice. Negotiations continued at speed, and were completed by November when, at a reunion Council meeting, Bishop Heddle, now 74 years old, delighted the gathered elders by vaulting over the table to extend the right hand of fellowship to the long-estranged Liberty brethren.

The terms on which the two parties had agreed to come together, were less clear. Differences over the main point at issue, the question of divine healing and medical aid, upon which the two parties had divided in the first place, had apparently been overridden. At the public reunion thanksgiving held with great rejoicing at Chelmsford in January 1921, the Liberty Church, according to one of its leaders, had agreed to concede absolutely:

> asking no terms, asking no favours, but with an unqualified surrender, prepared to go back to that position which we left in 1900[17].

This would seem to imply a return to the hardline rejection of medical aid then operating, which was almost unthinkable. In fact, what the Libertyites had agreed to, was the relevant clause of the Deed Poll concerning divine healing, a conflation of which was read out at the meeting, which clouds the essential point in a suitable vagueness:

> We agree that the whole tenor and scope of both the Old and New Testament Scriptures, which embody the will and commandments of God, as taught by His holy prophets, and that

of our Lord and Saviour Jesus Christ and His Apostles, do very clearly and distinctly set forth that God, the Creator, is the redeemer, Saviour and Quickener, Physician and Healer of all who fully believe and faithfully trust in Him through Christ Jesus, and that man's redemption from sin and his reconciliation and acceptance with God and also his deliverance from sickness and disease, is through faith in and by obedience to God's Word, also that the children are made partakers of the benefit of God's healing power, through the parents' faith and prayers, and also by the faith and prayers of others, and that we cannot declare the whole counsel of God, the mind and will of God, if we exclude the doctrine of faith healing, namely "the healing of sicknesses and diseases through faith in Jesus Christ", and such deliverances are the signs that confirm the Gospel, giving visible proof that the doctrine is of God[18].

This, after all, is far from being a bold reaffirmation of the rejection of medical aid! The complete absence of any assertion that divine healing must stand alone for the instruments of it to "declare the whole counsel of God", or that to seek the assistance of doctors is weakness and failure, tells its own story. In fact, this pronouncement, far from enumerating the concessions of the Libertyites, on the contrary contains an indication of how far William Heddle's party had moved towards the Liberty position in twenty years. The number of cases of the rejection of medical aid in the main church had indeed markedly declined since the War, and continued to decline. There could not be, except in the widest interpretation of the words, any "going back". Time and society and the Peculiar People had moved on.

And, even while total union was being celebrated, the first chapels of the Peculiar People were beginning to close: Upchurch in Kent, in 1920; Herongate not long surviving the death of its leading elder, William Shearman, in 1922; the Liberty church at Poplar in 1924. A mission founded by Brother Samuel Hammond further afield at Cambridge in 1921 (it used to meet upstairs at the White Ribbon Coffee Tavern), though placed on the Plan to fill the gap left by the demise of Upchurch, barely lasted five years. A mission founded by Brother Geary in Birmingham at about the same date, was, in that great and strange city, at best a forlorn hope. In 1922, Bishop Heddle was anxiously asking in Council: "Is the Church drifting into the world, or is the world draining into the Church?"[19], adding the awful question, as to whether "The Peculiar People" remained the church's correct title (the Council decided that it did). The threat from the Pentecostal movement had grown stronger than ever, meanwhile, and as the decade continued, several prominent Elders and Helps joined the flow of brethren to the new faith, the remonstrations of the Council (now amounting to five whole sheets of argument) notwithstanding: indeed, several Pentecostal groups in Essex and East London were actually founded by ex-members of the Peculiar People.

In response, a Forward Mission Movement was set up in 1923 with the somewhat ambitious aim of "advancing Holiness in the Church, and Evangelising the world". It was a scheme whereby specially talented ministers could be despatched at will to reinforce the work at churches that seemed to be ailing, in services of one or two weeks: they could also help to stimulate activity in the Sunday Schools. This having a certain success, in 1925 it was agreed to permit talented brethren not in the ministry to address these meetings, and this in turn led to the creation of an Itinerant Ministry (1927), utilising for the first time in many years the talents of the younger brethren which had lain dormant and neglected while the elders at each church had exercised an autocratic sway. (It was pointed out that in Bishop Harrod's day, this had not been the case: many young Brothers, though not ministers, had been sent out to conduct services, and fill Plans, taking their place in the preacher's desk at the churches they visited, though they never occupied the desk at home). The Itinerant Ministers would fulfil a kind of supplementary Plan: in time, work in the itinerant ministry came to be regarded as a necessary preparation for the ministry itself. A new fund and special services of exhortation for the Sunday Schools were also agreed.

At length, in 1929, the controversial decision was made, to admit evangelical missionaries from other denominations to speak in the chapels of the Peculiar People:

> Provided such meetings do not interfere with our regular or special services, And provided further that all such meetings should only be held by the consent of all the Elders of the Church concerned and that an Elder of the Peculiar People shall officiate at all such gatherings[20].

To a certain extent, this interdenominational communication had been proceeding unofficially for several years. The Liberty churches at Totham and Stanway in north Essex had remained "close" after the reunion, still looking to Edward Brazier as their leader, and these, with the People at Witham, had been noticeably forward in the later 1920s in encouraging contact with other religious groups, particularly Methodists and Baptists: to such an extent that their own services had taken on a markedly Methodist tone. They had also been anxious to discard what they regarded as the sillier aspects of Peculiarism (that is to say, its distinguishing features), and were in the forefront of those who objected to the heavily formal Sunday black, to the separation of the sexes in chapel, and to the absence of instrumental music. Their views on these subjects quickly permeated the whole movement, so that by the end of the next decade, the wearing of the quaint Peculiar's bonnet, for instance, had largely become confined to the older generation, and non-conformity, in dress at least, had all but disappeared.

Still chapels were closing: the church at Steeple, which had been failing for a number of years, in about 1933, and Gravesend at the same period. In fact, a church established at Eastwood near Southend in 1926 by Brother James Smith, builder, and Brother William Lewis, farmer, which still thrives, has the distinction of being the last successful mission of the Peculiar People to be planted.

In 1935, Edward Brazier, in a memorandum to the Council, suggested that further expansion of the movement could now be achieved only with the greatest difficulty, if indeed it was possible, and he listed his reasons: the lack of young converts to the faith, the ponderous bureaucracy of the Council itself, the lack of organic unity in the churches, the anachronism of such titles as 'bishop' and 'elder' (were they, in fact, not synonymous?): all failings which the Council readily acknowledged. He asked whether the church was right to maintain its position of isolation, in reply to which two recommendations were made by the Council:

> That we should recognise the present day work of the Holy Spirit who is undoubtedly calling all true believers into Close fellowship. That there is no call for a rash intermingling with all who take the name of Christ, But a definite call to "try the

spirits" and that we continue to impress upon our Members the great importance of loyalty to the calls of their own Church"[21]

The outbreak of the Second World War for a time prevented further developments in this direction.

At least, in the Second World War, there was no confusion about the church's position, as there had been in the First: the clear statement of non-involvement which had been agreed in 1919, was circulated to every chapel. But war did not bring increase any more than peace had done: in London especially, the bombings and evacuations physically wrought the destruction that, spiritually also, was being effected on all sides. At Silvertown the whole community was obliterated in the dockland bombings, while Canning Town was changed out of all recognition, though the chapel itself escaped destruction. Silvertown did not reopen after the War, and the post-War congregation at Tansley's old chapel settled down to about half its previous strength, with a corresponding decline elsewhere.

In 1946, a happier aspect of the long tradition was celebrated when the remarkable Bishop Heddle, still spry and fit, reached his hundreth birthday. Though he had officially retired from active duties in 1942, he still lived scrupulously according to Peculiar principles: since the day of his conversion in 1873, no doctor had ever been to attend him, nor had he taken pill, powder or plaster; nor, for that matter, eaten a cooked meal on a Sunday since that date. That he had thrived nevertheless, he demonstrated to a newspaper reporter who came to visit him, by jumping about his room. When he had first been converted, he remembered this town which now sprawled in all directions, as a collection of thatched cottages and farms, which a banker on horseback used to visit weekly from Rochford, Banyard's town. He had known the early leaders of the church, and shared in the decision making for over sixty years. With his removal from the scene, two years later, one more link with the past was severed.

In the 1950s, the church resumed the process of reconciliation, and the lowering of the sectarian barrier which had begun over twenty years before. Religion itself was now under attack, and many churches were seeking to combine, to present a common front in a secular society. 'Peculiarity' in its narrower sense now seemed less important when all were threatened: it was the truth the churches shared, rather than insignificant differences, that needed to be emphasised. For the Peculiar People, whose original base was so small, the problem was particularly pressing.

In 1955 the church began negotiations for affiliation to the Fellowship of Independent Evangelical Churches (F.I.E.C.), an organisation of 'Bible believing' Christians founded in 1922, with its headquarters in London. A meeting between the two bodies in May 1955, revealed that there was a considerable measure of agreement between them in matters of belief and common objectives. It was felt by both parties that it might well prove possible to unite upon the following basis: that the churches of the Peculiar People retained, at least for an interim period, their familiar organisation and entity as a group within the F.I.E.C; that each church of the Peculiar People be affiliated to the F.I.E.C., and that the three circuits form 'auxiliaries' after the manner adopted by the Fellowship, with each auxiliary gaining a representative on the Fellowship Council; that fully fledged ministers of the Peculiar People be accepted as accredited ministers of the Fellowship, but that all further candidates should comply with the requirements laid down by the Fellowship; and that the churches of the Peculiar People be renamed Evangelical Churches with the addition of the local designation in each case (e.g. 'Rochford Evangelical Church'). No alteration or modification of belief was called for.

On the 7th March 1956, the Elders' Council agreed to these changes, which were subsequently written into the Deed Poll. The Peculiar People had passed into history.

CHAPTER IV

Life and Worship

Brother Henry Sandford of Tillingham, a ploughman, speaking at one of the meetings of the Peculiar People in the early years of the century, recalled how on one occasion he was ploughing, and while going up the field was meditating on the goodness of God. When he got to the point where he must turn round, instead of calling out as usual to his horses, he shouted "Bless the Lord!" "My heart", he said, "was inditing a good matter." He praised God for His healing power: "Here I am today, a monument of mercy, spared to praise His glorious name. I have never had to pay one halfpenny for the help of medical man. I have found a Friend; He loved me ere I knew Him; He loved me when I was sin-pursuing, when I was fighting against Him; my Jesus has done all things well"[1].

Brother Elijah Everitt of Totham was another who had felt the blessing of the Lord while at his work. One day in 1879, Brother Everitt was expected to take a load of corn from Great Totham to Maldon; that meant very hard work in loading, he being a little man, and, as he was unwell, he dreaded the task. When he got to the barn that morning, he attended to his horses and waggon, but had to leave them outside the barn for some time, while he went to another part of the farm. When he returned, he found that some kind man had loaded the waggon for him, and all he had to do was to drive off. "While he meditated on this kind act, the Lord spoke to him, showing him that Jesus had paid his debt of sin, and all he had to do was to accept his offer of salvation; this he realised, and there and then, by faith, he ventured on Jesus, accepting him as his Saviour. Immediately he experienced the blessed change of being born again: and was filled with love, joy and peace. He rejoiced greatly in this blessed

experience, going in and out of the barn and round about,
praising the Lord. When he reached home that night his wife
(who had long been urging him to join the Peculiar People)
noticed a change in him, and when he told her what had
happened, they rejoiced and praised the Lord together"[2].

"They believe in instantaneous conversions", the local his-
torian Benton noted of the sect, "and relate at their meetings
how the Lord came to them when at the wash-tub, or sailing
in a barge, or whilst walking on a common &c". To Brother
William Wiffen of Prittlewell, the moment of conversion
came whilst engaged in one of the most tedious and weari-
some occupations of the old countryside, threshing in the
barn with a hand-flail. This experience, which relates to the
year 1846, was written down in 1918:

> When I was a lad just turned fifteen I came up from my home
> to the parish of Woodham Mortimer (three miles from Maldon).
> There I went harvesting with a man who was a Peculiar, and
> he told me about his People. Then I went to hear them in
> Bicknacre. There was a woman came into the Chapel that after-
> noon I was there; she had an affliction in her leg, so that she
> could only walk with the aid of a crutch and a stick; she attended
> the Order of laying on of hands in the Name of Jesus; the Lord
> blessed her and delivered her so that she went home carrying
> the crutch and stick under her arm. This made a great impres-
> sion upon me, and I went to the Chapel again in the evening.
> The People seemed so happy, and I thought I should like to feel
> as they did. They sang for the closing hymn, "Jesus descended
> to seek and save the lost". That hymn was upon my mind all
> night; the Spirit of God so worked upon me that I could not
> rest. The next morning, when I got up, I did not feel much like
> going to work; I had to do thrashing, but I was so troubled
> about my soul that I did not know how to do my work. I kept
> asking the Lord to tell me what I was to do. I wanted to get rid
> of my load of sin. I was miserable. I was afraid even to be in
> the barn alone, that morning. I got on my knees and prayed to
> the Lord that He might save me, and after I was willing to give
> up all, as the People of God had told me, I said to the Lord,
> "What more have I got to do? Show me". As soon as I said
> that, the Lord blessed me. By faith I saw them crucifying the
> Lord, and I felt His blood was running down for me. There
> was a light shone round me brighter than the sun. That was
> about ten minutes to nine on the Monday morning. The Lord
> saved me and made me extremely happy; I could thrash and

sing. Before that I was so miserable I hardly knew what to do with myself. When my mate came back from breakfast, he looked at me and said, "Mate, you are better than you were!" I said, "Yes, the Lord has saved my soul since you have been gone!" He said, "Praise the Lord!" Knowing the Lord himself, he praised the Lord with me[3].

As a contrast to the above, the following testimony of 1868, relates the experience of a brother living in Woolwich, a few years before the church there was involved in its healing controversy. This testimony was set down in 1913:

Forty five years ago and beforehand, I was greatly afflicted with tape worms, and was very weak, but with difficulty still kept to work. The doctors could not cure me. My "club" doctor was a clever doctor of great experience (he had been to the Crimean War). He tried his best to remove these worms from me, but without success. He told me that they had destroyed the digestive part of my stomach and that I would die a wretched death, for all the medicine in his shop would not cure me. Sometimes I got out of bed and walked the streets of Plumstead, for I could not rest. I felt I must die and go to Hell. I was at work about the Garrison and the Academy and Herbert Hospital, top of Woolwich Common.

The Peculiar People were preaching about Woolwich. Some of them came where I was at work. They used to preach in the Beresford Square. I reckoned and said I would hang the lot of them, if I had my will. I used to be spiteful against them.

My mate came to me one Monday morning, and said, "You must come along with me". I said "Where?" (thinking he meant to have a drink, for he was fond of drink). He said: "To go and hear the Peculiar People, for I went last night, and I thought I would have to praise the Lord". Those words seemed to sink right in me, for he whom I thought was a lot greater sinner than I was, for him to talk like that – true, he had told me before this that something had told him that he had only two years to live. He told how the People looked, and how a lot of them were navvies, but how nice they looked, and their wives also. So I agreed to go, and I went on the Wednesday night. After I came home my wife asked me what sort of people they were, and how they were dressed. I said, "A lot of them were navvies and their wives, but they do look happy, and the women with their little bonnets on, and their faces do shine". So my wife said, "If I live till Sunday, I won't cook dinner, I'll go and see them". But I wanted my cooked dinner. However, we both went and, after coming home, she said to me, "I wish

I was like them". I wished the same, and on the Wednesday night following we went again and they told us in their preaching if we believed Jesus was our Saviour, the Lord would save us. I got up and told them I believed Jesus was my Saviour and the Lord saved me.

The following Sunday we went again. I had an attack come on in the forenoon, the blood flying to my head as it used to do. Although I had been an entire stranger to them I went up to the platform and the Elder laid his hands on me in the name of Jesus Christ, and the people sang and praised the Lord. My wife was praising God, and her face shone beautifully; the Lord saved her, and the Lord healed me there and then.

I went to see the doctor afterward, and told him that the Lord had healed me. He said, "I don't want to say anything to it" (no more did he, although he always seemed to respect us). I have never had any physic or pills, powders or plasters since, and it is forty-five years ago next Sunday (the 8th November 1913). I am now eighty-two years of age. I can well recommend my Saviour, my Physician, my Healer, to one and all, rich and poor, for time and for eternity. Praise the dear Saviour. Hallelujah![4].

"For the most part their meetings are held in barns and other buildings of that character", wrote a correspondent to 'The Times' in 1888, "but by dint of considerable sacrifice, they have erected in one or two villages special places of worship, and here they have complete field-days on Sundays . . ."

The Peculiar People had four services on Sundays, at 6.30., 10.30., 2.30., and 6.30., following the pattern laid down by Banyard in the early days: those who could, would attend them all. This meant early rising, and a long day indeed for Elders "planned out" to some distant chapel. A brother with a donkey cart who went round to the house of Elder Thomas Rayner of Wakering at five o'clock on a Sunday morning to take him off to preach, and found him still in bed, chaffed him the rest of the day about it: "There's a preacher!" he said: "There's a preacher! Man going to preach the Gospel and he ain't even up!". On another occasion, Thomas Rayner told how he had cut a full acre of corn with the scythe on a Saturday, and yet had to be at Upchurch in Kent by 6.30 the next morning to preach, a schedule which even he thought was "going it a bit" (although he managed it).

Above: *Elder William Shearman of Herongate (see p.56) driving to chapel with his family*

Below: *Great Wakering Peculiars' Outing, 1906*

Above: *Rayleigh Sunday School outing, 1909*

Below: *A typical chapel interior*

Most of the journeying to chapel that was such a feature of the Peculiar's Sunday was, however, for the ordinary brethren, for the purpose of arriving at the 10.30 service, since only those close by could hope to be in chapel by 6.30. The country chapels being widely spaced, most members had considerable journeys on foot to undertake each Sunday; public transport, if available, was often scorned, and few had their own means to ride. So little family parties of Peculiars would be seen early out, passing through the fields and lanes on their way to chapel: the men in dark suits and bowler hats, the women in their inky black street-sweeping gowns, with black button-up boots, and close-fitting bonnets on their heads, tied under the chin with broad ribbons; the children restrained from leaping up and down banks and through hedges, as they would have been wont to do on any other day. Other parties, above hedge height, would be moving at a brisker pace, in a variety of horse-drawn traps and gigs.

"What takes place in their assemblies on Sundays, and on weekday evenings", wrote the Rev Canon Bateman, Rector of Southchurch in Essex in 1882, and a violent critic of the brethren, "can be easily imagined. But if the Peculiar People deny what I have been told, that at certain times *kissing between relations* is allowed, and that rooms are darkened to allow individuals to 'see Jesus', I shall be very glad. This I do know, that their services are sometimes very full, and sometimes very noisy and tumultuous . . ."[5].

The chapel doors being opened, in went the brethren on a Sunday morning, a plain whitewashed interior with the occasional text, and lamps hanging down overhead, being revealed. At the far end (the vestry door was to one side), the preacher's desk dominated the congregation: into the solid dark woodwork half a dozen elders would climb and take their places (the children facetiously called it "the waggon"). Below, hats and coats would be deposited on the interminable lines of hat pegs along the walls – the identical bowlers hung on each peg presented a curious spectacle of uniformity. The leather bags and baskets containing food for the midday meal would be placed in the vestry, where in winter a fire would be blazing, and where bowls of soup and meat pies were sometimes placed, to warm while the service was proceeding. Men and women then divided to left and right of the central gangway, and took their seats.

The Rev Canon Bateman would have been disappointed by the apparent order of the service: all went to a set pattern. First the Elder would rise to announce the hymn, which he read through in its entirety (a practice inherited from earlier times, when most of the brethren had been illiterate, and hymns had been dealt out in parcels of two lines, or at most a stanza at a time). The Elder strove to put as much expression as possible into the limping lines: for hymn singing was an important feature of these services. As soon as he had finished reading, the tune pitcher or precentor, would stand up with pitch pipe or tuning fork to establish the pitch, and with no further guide, the congregation launched into praise.

The first hymn of the Sunday morning service was followed by the laying on of hands for such sick persons as required it: they came forward and stood before the desk, where the Elder performed the Order, while the congregation sympathetically prayed or sang. If a "miracle" occurred, the chapel at once lit up with enthusiasm: in normal circumstances, the rite was naturally integrated into the service.

In preparation for prayer, the congregation turned about so that they were kneeling with their backs to the Elders, addressing their prayers in the direction of the chapel doors. Why they did this nobody seems to know, though one of my correspondents categorically states: "They turned towards the door, so that the Devil could not creep in unseen"[6]. Prior to kneeling, several of the men would ostentatiously produce large handkerchiefs which they spread out and laid upon the boards, to protect their best trousers. The women, on their side of the chapel, had cushions to kneel upon, which were left behind for use week after week.

The elders led in loud and fervent prayer and thanksgiving; another hymn followed, and then it was testimony time. A correspondent stresses the intimacy of the occasion:

> Sunday morning! Testimony time! What a happy time it was! We got to know each other in a very intimate way. We were taken into each other's everyday lives: how the Lord had helped them in their work and other ways. One I remember got up and said: "I felt very bad in the week; I thought I was going to die – but here I am! You don't always die when you feel bad",

he said. Another I remember trying to put across that he had
done with worldly things, said: "I took my pictures off the wall
and hung up my pitchfork" (This one worked on a farm). I
tried to imagine the bare walls with that pitchfork hanging
there. That was a bit extreme to me, but he rejoiced in the fact.
We were all expected to give our testimony: it gave the Elders
an insight into our spiritual growth.

Another correspondent conveys something of the atmosphere in which such testimonies were heard:

> I used to like to hear the morning service, when one of our
> brothers or sisters would stand up and testify to the Lord their
> thanks for helping them over some difficulty. Then all round
> the chapel you would hear: "Praise the Lord! Hallelujah!" and
> then some one would break into song: "Sing them over again
> to me/Wonderful words of love", or "This is my story, this is
> my song", and always finished up with
>> I will believe, I do believe
>> That Jesus died for me,
>> And on the Cross He shed His blood
>> From sin to set me free.
> By that time they would have danced and clapped their way all
> round the chapel.

Upon this note, the morning service ended. There was
then a short interval for lunch, for, in common with several
other sects, the Peculiar People ate in chapel. An informal
occasion this, with plenty of chatter among the open bags
of food, and a going hither and thither with cups of tea from
the vestry: it might have seemed a family outing on a picnic,
but for the clashing darkness of heavily formal clothes.

The afternoon service was generally more subdued, being
given over largely to preaching and Bible instruction by the
leading elder. Nevertheless, the congregation did not remain
silent, but followed the argument with many interjections,
sighs and other inimitable responses, as their faith was
renewed by fresh revelations. At least, most of them did: on
one occasion, a brother who fell asleep during a long sermon,
woke up suddenly with a start, and "Praise the Lord!" he
said. "I don't know what our brother's praising the Lord
about," the elder commented, "unless it's the nice sleep he's
had". This was an unusual remissness; by contrast, on
another occasion, so impassioned did the listeners become,

that when the elder paused in his discourse to take a glass of water, one of the brothers sitting below leapt to his feet and finished the sermon for him[7].

The afternoon meeting ended at 4.30. In the country districts, brethren who were horsemen on farms or had other animals to attend, would slip out early, removing their correct bowlers unerringly from the long line of pegs[8]. Others who had long journeys to make might leave early too, or as soon as the service had ended. Everybody else stayed on: indeed, numbers almost invariably increased for the last meeting of the day.

At the evening meeting, enthusiasm was expected to be at its height. The chapel then was crowded, and eyes shone with expectation and excitement. The hymns seemed to be sung louder and with more dramatic emphasis than before: with the very first one given out, hands would be clapping, and feet stamping on the floor; the choruses were pounded out. Every hymn at this meeting was familiar, and every brother had his favourite verse, which he would have been determined to make the congregation repeat, by bellowing out its first line as they prepared to advance to the next stanza. They generally would follow his lead; and even if they did not, he might still continue, abstractedly pacing about and calling out the words (this was called "getting a blessing"). As the excitement mounted, ordinary restraints were set aside: members leapt from their places, ran and marched about, shook hands and patted shoulders, some with tears in their eyes, and some with faces filled with smiles. One or two brothers and sisters might even have dashed across the central aisle to embrace (I do not think, however, that the room was ever darkened!), and some certainly danced in their exhilaration, while the singing continued. A newspaper reporter who attended a meeting of Peculiars at Woolwich in 1905, noted, with nice precision, that a hymn of nine verses, with refrain and repeats, occupied the congregation for twenty-nine minutes of singing time:

> Each member commenced on a different note, yet some slight harmony was obtained towards the close, although this was lost in the wild clapping of hands and stamping of feet and dancing indulged in after the first few verses[9].

At a similar pitch, the preacher, expanding on his text, exhorted any poor lost souls that may have been present, to come to Jesus, a sentiment which the congregation heartily echoed, looking meaningfully at the strangers among them, and encouraging those they had brought with them, to praise the Lord. Then again the singing would start, and as the evening wore on, hymn followed hymn, one rising out of another at the insistence of some lone singer. This was the moment that some had been waiting for, if the weight of sin and guilt lay heavy upon them. Here is Brother Jesse Horsnell of London, converted at 16. "When I was about eight, there was a lot of us boys, and I said to one of them, 'You give your heart to the Lord, and I will' – but it doesn't happen like that. Eight years after the same boy, stepping off the shore onto a boat, fell in the water and was drowned. His body was found six weeks later. This brought an awareness of unpreparedness". A few months later, Jesse attended an evening meeting of Peculiars at the London church. Two hundred people were standing, and singing with gusto, the hymn, "Alas! and did my Saviour bleed? And did my Sovereign die?" Jesse, unable to keep back the tears streaming off his cheeks, had to sit down. Elder Thomas Gentry, the minister, saw it, and contrived that the last verse of the hymn, appropriate to his case, should be repeated: it was:

> But drops of grief can ne'er repay
> The debt of love I owe;
> Here, Lord, I give myself away,
> 'Tis all that I can do.

When it was finished, the minister turned to Jesse. "Young man, open your mouth!" Jesse says: "I had a job to get it out, but I knew what to say: *He's my Saviour!*" (he throws up his hand). "I was a lump of lead one moment and light as a feather the next: quick as the lightning!"

At the sight of one soul saved, the joy of the congregation knew no bounds, and the hymn singers redoubled their efforts: perhaps there may be another! At all accounts the long service would be brought to an end only with the greatest reluctance. When forced at length to break up the circle and go out into the night, the brethren would still regroup on the street corner for another chorus, and could have been heard long after dark, singing and praising in the lanes as they made their way towards home and their beds.

The faith of the new convert would soon have been tested. Outside the Totham chapel, the country people might warn him of the dire powers of those within: "Don't go in there: they put stuff on the floor to overpower you". Or at Rochford, the next Sunday, children might have shouted, as they sometimes did: "Hallelujah, I'm a Peculiar!" and have flung handfuls of mud over the hedge onto his Sunday clothes. Brother Stephen Owers of Witham, converted in 1880, had to endure "a wonderful persecution in the first few years of his new life", "in so much that once his life was threatened; but his reply was, 'If you kill me, home to Glory I shall go!' Once he was locked in the house, to prevent him going to chapel; but, asking God to help him, he touched the lock and it slipped back, and he went to the Meeting"[10]. Brother Thomas Whale of Great Wakering, a horseman, was another who suffered similarly: he at the hands of a cynical and ungodly workmate. On one occasion, Brother Whale was walking absentmindedly with a loaded dung cart; the horse, which he should have been leading, pulled ahead and knocked down a gate-post. A few days later his opponent laid his hand on his shoulder: "Ah brother," he said, "we need a guide on this earth, don't we?" Brother Whale replied solemnly: "Yes, mate, we do". "Yes, brother, we need a guide on this earth", the cynic continued, "to take us straight through the pearly gates so as we don't hit the post". Brother Whale always said the man had a very bitter feeling against him, and worked against him, and had even threatened him bodily harm. But one day, whilst they were together in the open, a heavy thunderstorm came on, and this gave Whale an opportunity which he was quick to embrace. To use his own words: "My mate had no coat, and tried his best to cover himself with hay. I had a big coat with a cape. I said to him: "Mate, I'll keep you dry; I'll see you don't get wet in the storm". I stood over him like a hen over her chickens and sheltered him from the storm. The man after that was never any more trouble to me. I could speak right. I could do anything almost, it was all right. He would even give me the things that I wanted . . ."[11]

The brethren, new converts and seasoned members, sure

of their faith, were earnest proselytizers, and seized every opportunity to advance their religion. To the Rev Canon Bateman, their zealous attentions almost amounted to persecution in reverse:

> I would say to the troubled, "Do not listen to their words, and do not accept their invitations. A Church principle is involved, and it is as easy to say 'no' as 'yes'. Let well alone. Nothing is perfect. The Church is not perfect: and you may be well assured that the Peculiar People are not! Throw earnestness and reality into that sentence of our Lord's Prayer: Lead us not into temptation"[12].

Brother Isaac Fryatt, one of the pioneer brethren who had carried the religion to Totham in the 1880's, used to go over to the allotments there, to chat with the men as they worked, and try to convert them. One was a Congregationalist: Brother Fryatt said to him: "If there's three shops: one's good, one's better, and one's best of all – which would you go to?" The man innocently said: "Why the best of all, of course". "Well", said Brother Fryatt, "You go to the Peculiar People!" Brother George Wiles of Cressing, who was of the same generation, was gunning with fierce determination for a "real bad man" who lived in his district. One day he saw him coming towards him on the road, and determined to stop and challenge him, and have a good talk. The poor man for his part saw Brother Wiles, and feared to face him: he knew what was coming! So, as they approached, he shrank to the side of the road, and at last crawled past him in the bottom of the ditch!

The considerable awe in which many simple people held the Peculiar People is not altogether surprising, considering the extraordinary powers they claimed by faith to possess. And not only the power of divine healing: they trusted, even in times of desperate need, that God would provide for them, and safeguard them, and if necessary, feed and clothe them too. For instance:

> A Brother and Sister were in great poverty, and came to the point where they had neither food nor firing. In the morning, the Sister said she would not rise from her bed, as it was no use getting up when there was no food for them. The Brother, however, rose, believing that God would provide for them. He prayed to God to help them, then set the breakfast, and presently

opened the door. Outside, he found a parcel, which contained just what they needed, even to wood and coal for the fire.[13]

Such stories circulated widely. Another is told of an old couple, in dire need of food, yet trusting in God. Although they had no tea in the house, they put the kettle on, feeling sure their need would be supplied. Sure enough, ere it boiled, there came a knock at the door, by one who had brought a good breakfast with her! Another instance is recalled by a correspondent:

> I remember on one occasion, I was told by one of the elderly brothers, that when he was a boy, his father died, and his mother was left a widow with her two sons. She had nothing to eat. He remembers his mother getting on her knees, pleading with God to send food to her boys. There came a knock on the cottage door: she got off her knees, and there was a man with a dead duck: "Here you are," he said. Oh how thankful she was – a real answer to her prayer. He said mother made that last all the week. He said, much later they heard the full story: how two men were shooting ducks: three of them got caught in the marshes. They shot all three, and one said to the other, "There's one for you, and one for me. Who shall we give this one to?" and they decided to give it to his mother, and brought it to her door, at the right time.

Canon Bateman condemned as a "deadly error" the fatalism into which, in his opinion, the brethren descended in such straits, and more notably, of course, their similar attitude towards the sick among them, if the powers of divine healing appeared to fail. He cites the case of one of his own parishioners, a strong healthy man, 58 years old, who was threatened with inflammation of the lungs from a common cold. Being a Peculiar, he sought the church's assistance: hands were laid upon him, and he was anointed with oil. Still he got worse, and eventually took to his bed. Bateman visited him, and tried to persuade him to see a doctor: he refused, since, he said, the Lord might raise him up if he pleased. His wife refused: "The Lord knows best", she said. A sister of the sect, who stood by, folded her arms: "It is the Lord's will," she said. When Bateman attempted to pray for the man, dying as he now perceived, he again refused:"I will not let you pray with me, or for me; I do not want your prayers. I have not done anything wrong for fifteen years.

I am a child of God: you are not. I will not hear a word you say." And he folded the bedclothes about his head and ears and turned away. With sorrow in his heart, Bateman was obliged to leave the house prayerless, and the man died within three days[14].

Other brethren in apparently good health, receiving a strong premonition of their own deaths, accepted it with similar calmness and resignation: a correspondent writes: "I remember one of our dear Elders . . . was taken ill, and said he had a vision of the Golden gates and his beautiful Home. He said how much he would have loved to have stayed there. After that he often spoke about it. He never forgot it. He used to have us sing the hymn 'My beautiful Home'. Months later he suddenly announced one Sunday evening that he wouldn't be there the following Sunday. To me, I couldn't believe it, he seemed so well, but he went around shaking hands with all, and by the next Sunday he had gone to that 'beautiful Home' ". In the same frame of mind, loving parents allowed their children to die, if the Lord did not see fit to raise them up.

A funeral of the Peculiar People was a grand affair. The body of the deceased would be laid out in his own home, as was at one time the general custom. The funeral procession began at the very door, the coffin, good but neat ("devoid of all wreaths or flowers, and with no outside display of unnecessary crêpe or black"), sometimes being placed on trestles before the house, so that prayers could be said, before proceeding to the chapel on the shoulders of four brethren. The mourners would fall in behind, sometimes as many as 150 or 200 brethren in lines of four, advancing slowly through the streets or down the country lanes. At the chapel the services would be prolonged; at the graveside, longer still, with continual singing of hymns around the grave. An hour or two might pass thus. A witness describes the atmosphere:

To go to a funeral service or to stand around the grave of one who had passed on, was like being at a Revival Service: they rejoiced in the fact that one had landed safely on the other shore. "In the sweet bye-and-bye/ We shall meet on that beautiful shore", they used to sing lustily. This used to make me sad as a girl. As I stood outside Mother's back door, you could hear

their voices ringing over the air. As I got older I could understand their joy, but as a child I could not enter into these things.

There was, surprisingly, only one burial ground for the
Peculiar People, a piece of land attached to the Daws Heath
chapel, obtained in 1882, where Bishop Harrod and many
members of his flock lie. The other chapels, further afield,
buried their dead in Church of England churchyards and in
cemeteries. By a strange irony, a doctor's certificate had to
be obtained to certify the death, though they would let no
doctors near them in their lives.

If the new member's attitudes towards life and death were
deeply affected by joining the church, his life itself was
moulded by the pattern of the church year, with its meetings,
services and festivals. The main meetings, apart from the
normal chapel services, were the Tea Meetings (afternoon
service 3 – 5; evening service 6.30 – 9), which were held on
public holidays. Christmas was celebrated with a greater
solemnity than is usual in English households, much of the
afternoon and the evening being spent in chapel in prayer,
praise and thanksgiving (the children opened their presents
on Christmas morning). In some parts, carol singing on
Christmas Eve was conducted with great fervour, though
no collection was taken: in Canning Town, they started at
about 10 pm, and went right through the night, ending at
5 am on the Christmas morning, with a special prayer meeting in chapel. Watch Night Tea Meetings on New Year's
Eve were also rather special: they began at about 3 in the
afternoon with tea, and a meeting; the evening meeting
began at 6.30 and lasted until 12.30 into the New Year, with
a break at about 10 o'clock. Easter Tea Meetings were held
with similar enthusiasm.

The great meetings of each year, however, were undoubtedly those connected with the harvest, the most important
event in the country calendar, and a period of work upon
which, in the earlier days, the whole economy of a household
could depend. In July or early August, pre-harvest meetings
would be held in chosen centres in each circuit of the Peculiar
churches – special services that were perhaps unique to the
denomination. They were the counterpart of the preparations
that the more ordinary labourers made before entering into
the harvest, which consisted in dosing themselves up with

physic and quack remedies (for there was no social security in those days, if a man fell ill). The Peculiar harvestmen went to chapel, and offered up praise to God for what he had already provided, prayers and intercessions that the weather might hold, and the crops do well, and desired that they and their animals might be preserved through the arduous days ahead. Practical advice was also offered at these meetings: brethren were warned to be sure that loads were properly secured, that the ladders for stacking were really long enough, to take care with the scythe, and with the machinery also, for this was a busy time, and notable for accidents.

A good harvest could be taken in a month, with the men organised into harvest companies, with a company leader or "lord" at their head. He, being the strongest man, set the pace for the line of reapers, and also negotiated terms with the farmer (all harvesting was done on a piecework basis). The days were long and the work all-embracing: in 1913, old Brother Bowtle of Tillingham recalled how, when a boy, he had to get into the harvest field before 5 a.m., and stopped out at night till 7. "In those days the poor man had to go, and his wife with him, and the children to follow on; everyone that could do a little had to do it". Brother Sandford, the Tillingham ploughman, had also known what it was to have his wife and children behind him in the harvest field while he swung the scythe. They had to gather into sheaves the corn he had cut, and bind it with straw ropes and pile it in stooks to dry: soon their hands and arms would be scratched and cut with the sharp grasses. Breakfast in the harvest field was at eight, and lunch was at two o'clock – each break lasting three-quarters of an hour: there were also quarter-hour breaks at 11 and 4; otherwise the march of the reapers across the white fields was uninterrupted all day long. For all this labour of a month or six weeks, a man might earn £8 or £9, with a harvest supper and beer *ad libitum*: Brother Bowtle told how some at the end of the harvest were not so well off as when they went in. Nevertheless, it was far more than could be earned on the land at any other time of the year, and it did provide an opportunity, for certain careful purchases, and the payment of long-standing debts. There was also, when the fields were cleared, the gleaning, which could bring in a surprising quantity. One certain harvest year, Brother John Hockley informs us, his mother and brothers and sisters gleaned in all 20 bushels of grain from the fields, which they took to the miller to be ground, and which supplied the household with "many a hard dumpling that winter and homebaked bread, and short-cakes, and plain pudding food, which we all enjoyed – which was all the great goodness of the Lord"[15].

For the Peculiar People, harvest was followed by the annual thanksgiving, the one time of the year when the whole church, or a great part of it, could unite its several chapels under one roof – a celebration that was also an after-harvest holiday. An air of festivity always hung over the occasion of the harvest thanksgiving: no fruit or flowers were in evidence, merely the brethren and their wives and children, streaming into the county town on one day of the year, to sing and pray and praise together – like an invasion of black beetles, as someone uncharitably described this annual event. Here is how one newspaper reported the pro-ceedings in 1887:

> In accordance with their usual custom, the Peculiar People held their united thanksgiving services at Chelmsford on Monday last, and from morning till night the town was alive with visi-tors belonging to that sect, gathered from far and near, to celebrate their greatest festival of the year. They came in by break (horse-brake), on foot, and in loaded waggons from remote districts, and heavily-laden trains from Colchester and the Metropolis, to which the intermediate stations contributed a good quota, all testifying to the hearty zeal and earnest enthusi-asm of a body of people who, with all their peculiarities, are a living religious power in this and the adjacent county of Kent. The majority of the Peculiars are unmistakably "horny-handed sons of toil" – such men as would have stood side by side with Cromwell in a struggle against the unreal and insincere in religion and morality. Their women-folk – many of them – wear a curious piece of head-gear, remarkable for its simplicity and its implied contempt for the latest Paris fashion. To the ordinary spectator it was an interesting experience to witness the hearty, unconventional greetings of brethren and sisters who probably had not had the pleasure of meeting since last harvest thanksgiving day. A deal of business was transacted in the town before the services began, the members as a rule taking advan-tage of their visit to the county town to lay in a stock of clothing

and other goods. At several points flags were flying with the intent of conveying in silent but pathetic language that refreshments were to be had within. Nearly every chapel in the connexion had representatives present at the proceedings, some coming from Kent and London, but most from the Dengie and Rochford Hundreds, where the Peculiar People are strongest. Luncheon was provided at the Corn Exchange, in the Boardroom by Mr Joseph Hicks, and immediately afterwards a move was made for the Baddow-road (Congregationalist) Chapel, which had been placed at the disposal of the management for the afternoon service. The building was packed – even the aisles being filled – early comers whiling away the time by singing some of their rousing hymns set to quaint tunes, in which repetitions are, to a stranger, a bewilderment and a snare. Babies this year seemed quite as numerous as on any previous occasions, almost every mother carrying one; and the devotions were accompanied by the wails and cries of infants[16].

The afternoon service was customarily devoted to discourse on the natural harvest by speakers who had practical knowledge of that, and thanks were gratefully raised for a year's early promises fulfilled. In the evening, the harvest theme was spiritualised, and discourse turned from the harvest past to the harvest to come, when "angel reapers shout the harvest home". Declarations of faith were made with great vigour and in good humour and in plain speech: though the meeting was supposed to be led from the platform, it was sometimes very difficult to control, for excitable brethren, bursting to speak, had a habit of rising in the centre of the hall to tell out the circumstances of their own conversions, exerting their voices and vigorously throwing their arms about, to the amusement of the uninitiated. To labourers who had just been through the harvest, the rural imagery of the Bible, now as always, had a wonderful significance, and convinced them that their religion was right and the scriptural experience was theirs. "Paul spoke as we did: I am sure of that," said one speaker, and "How can we contain ourselves after what God has done for us?" said another. The cheerful appearance of the celebrants, the absence of all cant from their speech, the rambling hymns in which the singers seemed to lose themselves in puffs of exaltation and delight, all told the same story: that for this generation, at

least, the life of work and the life of worship were not
separate, but one.

In later years, constraints and refinements entered: brethren were taught that to stamp the feet in public worship was
considered improper and should be avoided: the harvest sea-
son lost its significance, interruptions from the floor were
too easily quelled, the sense of a communal experience faded.
Then the great harvest meetings were less well attended, and
in time the people of Chelmsford were disturbed and
diverted by them no more.

CHAPTER V

Divine Healing

Some of the earlier cases of divine healing among the Peculiar People have already been related. In later years the ritual of healing became a regular part of the morning service on Sunday. After the first hymn, before engaging in prayer, those wishing to be healed would come forward to the front of the desk. The elder would come down out of the desk, and lay his hand upon the patient's head and pray for God to heal him. For those persons seriously ill, the full order, with anointing with oil on the afflicted part, would be carried out. The congregation would then join in with fervent prayer, asking God to intercede for the sick person.

There were instant healings of a spectacular nature in chapel. Bishop James Southgate, successor to Daniel Tansley at Canning Town, recalled how

> . . . a sister came one day on crutches and said she believed God would heal her. Our leader (now in heaven we believe) laid hands upon her in the name of Jesus and while he did so we were asking God to heal her, and God healed her: one crutch went one way, one the other, and she was leaping up and down the chapel; she went home without the crutches, and did without them[1].

A correspondent remembers that these crutches hung in the chapel for many years after, as a witness to the permanence of the cure. A similar case was recorded at Herongate, though the sufferer's disease is not specified:

> It is with great pleasure we make known a great and speedy deliverance, wrought on a poor woman by the power of God. This dear woman had been very ill during the week, but she feared and loved God and many times God had heard and answered her prayers and she felt that God could and would if she could get to the chapel on Sunday. She was conveyed in a

cart to the Peculiar People's chapel at Herongate. While there she was taken much worse and said she must die. During the afternoon the preacher spoke about the woman who touched the hem of Jesus' garment; this increased her faith, she believed God would heal her and make her well and strong. Her faith was rewarded; while the preacher was telling forth the mighty power of God to heal, the power of God entered her body, she leaped from her seat and ran about the chapel, healed perfectly, praising God with all her heart, soul and strength. The cure was a permanent one, from that day until her death, which was many years later, she was able to get about, and did a lot of hard work, living until she was seventy-eight years of age[2].

In most cases, the moment of healing is described as being marked by a feeling of power, and of warmth flowing through the body. The sensation is described in almost identical language in a variety of cases. One man said, "I fail to describe fully the beautiful glowing feeling which entered my head and went right down to my feet"; a woman called her own sensation of healing "such a beautiful heavenly feeling; it went right through me. It was as though somebody took a basin of warm oil and poured it over my body, from my head to my feet". And another man, healed when Tansley laid hands upon him, "felt the Power enter his head and go down to the soles of his feet."

The ceremony that took place on Sunday mornings in chapel could be performed anywhere on those who had faith, with equal power. There are even cases where unconscious people and small children, those, that is to say, oblivious to faith, or not sustained· by it, were healed in this way. One story concerns Brother Freddie Clarke, who had a fish shop in Canning Town. Hearing that a child had a foot "twisted right round" so that he could not stand on it, Clarke went to the house, still wearing his shop apron. Holding the foot in his cupped hands, he prayed over the child, and as he prayed, it is said the foot came round in his hands, and the child was healed. Brother H. Nicholas also of Canning Town, seems to have been used by God in the same way:

> One of his fellow workmen, a bad character, fell ill, insomuch that he took to his bed, and was thought to be dying. When Brother was going home to tea one day a policeman met him and requested him to go and see this man . . . When he arrived at this man's house, the room in which he was lying was full

tle Totham Evan-
lical Church,
ened 1890

The later chapel at Daws Heath, used until 1976

e chapel at Wick-
rd, opened 1912

ELDERS OF THE PECULIAR PEOPLE.

A PLAN
1874-5.

		NOV. 15	22	29	DEC. 6	13	20	27	JAN. 4	11	18	25	FEB. 1	8	15	22	MARCH 1	8
A	DAWS' HEATH																	
B	LONDON																	
C	HERON-GATE																	
D	WOOLWICH																	
E	PRITTLEWELL																	
F	WAKERING																	
G	WICKFORD																	
H	TILLINGHAM																	
I	STEEPLE																	
J	FOULNESS																	
K	WITHAM																	
L	STANFORD																	
M	BADDOW																	
N	UPCHURCH																	
O	CANNING TOWN																	
P	RIVENHALL																	

PROSPERITY.

EXHORTATION.

J. FRANCIS & SON, Printers and Bookbinders, Rochford and High Street, Southend, Essex.

Elders' Plan, 1874-5; notes by Bishop Samuel Harrod

of people, friends and relatives, waiting to see the last of him, thinking that he was about to die. A nurse stood at his bedside, holding his wrist with one hand and a gold watch in the other, waiting for life to be extinct. Brother made his way to the bedside and asked the nurse if he could lay hands upon him. She refused. Brother then asked if she would allow him to lay his hands on the outside of his clothes. This he did, and the man sat up, the people in the room being of course greatly surprised. The next morning the doctor called, and as the man's daughter opened the door, he said: "Your father is dead, isn't he?" "Oh no" she replied, "A Peculiar came here last night and laid hands upon him and he is better!" The doctor of course could hardly believe it, but on seeing the man pronounced him out of danger – "Peculiar or no Peculiar", he remarked[3].

The same man was instrumental in the case of others who were not of the faith:

> Brother was going home to dinner one day when a man met him and asked him to go and see his daughter who was seriously ill. Brother promised to go after he had dinner. So he went, and when he got there the young woman was indeed very ill. He took her hand and talked gently to her, and then laid his hands on her and prayed for her, and she sat up and called downstairs for a new-laid egg to be brought to her. God delivered her. As brother was coming downstairs, the mother of the woman met him and said: "The doctor gave her baby up last night." Brother said: "Is the baby ill too?" "Yes" she replied. "Oh", he said, "God can heal the child as well; may I see it?". So he was allowed to see the baby, and he laid his hands on it in the name of the Lord, and God healed it, and it lived and grew a fine child[4]".

In the majority of cases, however, the faith of the sufferer was a major factor in the effectiveness of the cure.

The elder did not necessarily have to be present for the healing to take place. Sometimes the power was transmitted through the agency of a handkerchief. In one case it is stated briefly that a girl who had lain severely ill and who had not spoken for a month, was raised again to health by a handkerchief being applied to her from him who had first prayed over it[5]. The second case is given in a little more detail: it was related by Brother George Harrod of Southend. He

> quoted the case of one sister who was taken very ill, some two or three years ago; they did not know what the affliction was,

but the sister was in such pain at times that she hardly knew what to do with herself. Another sister visited her, and urged her to try the means as the Apostle tried, to send a handkerchief; she sent the handkerchief to Brother Harrod, and he laid it before the Lord (as we read of one who laid a letter before the Lord – see Isaiah xxxvii, 14). He would never forget his experience when on his knees; the beautiful heavenly virtue and feeling that came to him was such that he was satisfied God would heal her. He then sent the handkerchief back in the name of the Lord, and when it was applied to the sister's body God healed her there and then.[6]

It is remarkable here that it was the elder and not the sufferer, who experienced the "beautiful heavenly . . . feeling" associated with the healing process. Unfortunately, no more is known of this cure which presents, in outline, such an intriguing picture to the imagination.

It may be thought that these healings were stimulated, and may even have occurred through strong collective emotions, such as would be generated by a sympathetic congregation, but a surprising number of healings among the Peculiar People happened to people entirely alone and unaided, whose sincerity cannot be doubted. Brother George Anderson of Barking is a case in point:

He had been unwell for a long time, and one evening while sitting against the fire he heard something say, "He won't heal me now", but a feeling was revived in his breast, and the thought came, "He will", and he was healed at once. He felt the power. It was not through excitement, as he was all alone[7].

In certain cases, as for instance when one of the Bishops fell ill, special days of fasting and intercessory prayer were held in all the churches of the Peculiar People. This was a recognised practice among the People. Certain healings were attributed to the power generated by these united prayers. Brother E. Whipps of Steeple cut his thumb while using a chaff cutter:

Soon the inflammation ran up his arm, and he was not able to use it. On the Thursday evening, he sent to the chapel (at Steeple), asking his brethren to pray for him. At the time he thought they were praying, he anointed it with oil in the name of the Lord Jesus Christ, and the Lord healed it, so that he went to the House of the Lord the following Sabbath[8].

In another case, intercessory prayer and healing are directly linked: again, the sufferer, Brother Caleb Rayner (who had diptheria) is alone, and the sympathetic agency is at a remove:

> I had become very low in so much my life was despaired of; nothing had passed my lips for several days, could not even swallow my own spittle, and was unable to speak. In addition to this I had four little children (the oldest being six years old) all down with the same disease, so mine was a sad case. There were some people about, who knowing I refused medical aid, were not exactly friendly and by some means the doctor had been informed of our plight, and I then received a letter from him on a particular Thursday saying he would call the next morning at 10 o'clock. Thursday was meeting night at the Chapel, so I motioned for pencil and paper and requested special prayer. Two brethren came but could not anoint me just then, having no oil with them. However, my request was known to God. I was given the words:
>
> > "The Lord has promised good to me,
> >   His word my hope secures,
> > He will my shield and portion be
> >   As long as life endures."
>
> Whilst my brothers and sisters were praying, the Lord healed me suddenly – in a flash. I could immediately speak and partook of a good meal. Praise the Lord! I asked my dear mother, who was with me, to go along to the Chapel. Just outside were some people who knew of my condition, and seeing her, asked: "Is your son gone?" "No" she said, "the Lord has healed him." When the news reached our friends, the meeting was turned from a prayer to a praise meeting, as has been the case more than once."[9]

We are introduced to yet another twist in the remarkable thinking of the Peculiar People on this subject. We might well ask: Why should they have been so terrified of the doctor? There is no basis in the Bible for such a fear, and yet many had a dread so deep it might almost be thought that they considered doctors as agents of the devil. The testimony just quoted continues:

> My trouble was not ended for there were the children and there was the letter which I then read again. This was a wonderful time and the faith was given me, and I grasped it, to say without doubt, "The Lord has healed me, and he will heal my children,

and we shall all be downstairs before 10 o'clock in the morning." The work was done, the children were all healed in their sleep, and before 10 o'clock the next morning we were all downstairs. The doctor arrived and was obliged to say he could see nothing amiss with any of us. God has completed the work and we are all alive today. To Him be all praise!".

An even more extreme reaction to doctors and medicine was shown by Brother George Carey of Daws Heath, who, after a fall in which he was badly injured, was given a letter to admit him to Guy's Hospital. "But" said the old man "I thought it was like going to the gallows." "His mind was in a fearful state of worry, and one Sunday morning he got out of bed and prayed: in a very short time he heard a silent whisper, which he knew was from the Lord, saying: "Go to Daws Heath and get healed". He was then living at Battlesbridge, but he got up and started out at once, walking seven miles to the place where the Lord had told him to go. When he got there he told Bishop Harrod of his trouble, and the Bishop laid hands on him and prayed for him, asking another Elder at the same time to do likewise. "From that time" (said Brother Carey, joyfully) "I got well, and a week after I was quite healed. So what the skill of man could not do the Lord accomplished . . ."[10].

Mention here of the "silent whisper" reminds one of the many times an apparently divine command lead the instrument of healing to the sufferer. Here are two further instances. The first concerns Brother William Wood, the leader at Rochford after Banyard's death: one of his church members fell ill: the sufferer's grandson writes:

My grandfather (Brother Barnes) was sick in bed with a fever and during the harvest time his help was vital. Brother Wood was chopping firewood at home when a voice said: "Go and see so-and-so": the voice was persistent. So away he trudged across the fields, not really knowing in which direction the house was. However, he saw a light in the distance, and after knocking, my grandmother said "Oh! it's Brother Wood! We were praying you would come." As soon as his foot touched the first step to go upstairs, my grandfather, lying in bed, felt his fever leave him. He was up and out working the next day"[11].

In another case a similar directive was received by Brother Sidney Holmes of Chadwell Heath:

Early one morning this young man was hoeing in a field near Chadwell Heath station, meditating on the goodness and love of God . . . Whilst so engaged, a voice spoke to him, saying, "Go to Barking", to a brother who was very ill and suffering from quinsies and pleurisy, unable to raise himself in bed; he had heard that the brother was unwell, but did not know whether he had recovered or not. He obeyed the voice, which also said, "Go, doubting nothing, and I will make my power manifest". He thought for a little time when he should go; he thought he would go at dinner time, seeing it was a considerable distance, but could not seem to get on with his work, and the word "Go" kept revolving in his mind; he laid down his hoe, and said, "Lord, I will go *now*"; off he went in the name of Jesus. Reaching the house he was received by the brother's wife, who said her husband was upstairs in bed, and asked him to see him. When he entered the room he saw the brother was in pain and great need, and told him the Lord had sent him, and he had come for God to heal him. The brother said, "Praise the Lord; if the Lord has sent you, brother, He is sure to heal me; get on with what God has told you". He then laid his hands on him and prayed to God to deliver him; the brother said, "Do, Lord". There and then God took the pain away; in a short time he was able to turn in bed; the next day he got up and dressed himself, for God had healed him[12].

To attempt to interpret these and other accounts of healings by scientific means, is obviously impossible, especially as in many cases, even the diseases have not been diagnosed. Sometimes, at least, certain supposed miracles might be questioned. For instance, Brother William Bridge of Tillingham claimed as the first proof of divine healing he had had, the following:

About two months after his conversion, his child spilt a saucer full of hot milk down his breast. A brother came in and poured oil over the breast and the child left off crying at once[13].

It is not unlikely that oil might have a soothing effect on a mild burn.

In another case, a young Brother at Wakering, passing through a shed on his way to work, caught his foot in a chaff cutter belt and, falling, gashed open the palm and wrist of one hand upon a knife standing in the corner of the room, sharpened ready for use.

He had friends around him, for someone bound his hand up,

and one of the workmen would have taken him to the doctor. But the young lad . . . had seen what great things the Lord Jehovah had done for his parents through faith in Jesus' Name, so he went to his father (who was working near by), who took him home, and whilst crossing the fields to the street, the blood streamed from the boy's hand. He began to look very white . . . .Just as they left the field, they saw one of the Elders (Brother Rayner) in the street, and oh how glad they were. When he saw what was the matter, he followed father and son indoors, where the lad was quickly laid on the sofa, for he had almost lost consciousness. He had just enough strength to say, "Lay your hands on me, please, Mr. Rayner, and ask the Lord to help me". This he readily did, asking the Lord to stay the flow of blood and remove the pain. In answer to prayer the Lord immediately did so, and neither returned for some time, although till then the blood was spurting through the rag like a fountain. Shortly after a sister and a kind neighbour came to bind the wound afresh, and when they removed the former binding, the wound did not bleed very much . . .[14]

The incident is more valuable as illustrating the resolution of the People in a crisis, than as an example of miraculous healing.

Sometimes, especially where diseases of nervous origin are concerned, it is possible to see a supposed miracle in psychological rather than in purely spiritual terms. In the following case, which was given some publicity at the time, we enter a more shadowy region, where many factors seem to act upon one another to resolve a crisis. The woman in question was a Sister Outen of Fobbing:

"For six years" she said, "I was afflicted with an internal trouble which at times rendered me quite helpless. I was frequently advised to go into a hospital, but I did not do so until four years ago last January. I then went to the London Hospital, but I came out feeling worse than when I went in. I was advised by doctors to go back to the hospital, but during that time a little Peculiar's chapel was opened at Fobbing, and I attended the opening services. In my distress I continued to attend the chapel, and a week later, on the 13th March 1910, the Lord opened up my life as if it were in a book. I saw the promises and professions I had made, and it seemed to me that as the Lord was reading that book I had to make a final venture. It was my last chance. I was taken terribly bad in that place, and I felt that I should never come out alive if I did not make a surrender to Christ.

Brother John Hockley was preaching, and he was using the words, 'This is your last chance.' While he was talking I raised my eyes to the corner of the chapel, where there seemed to be a glorious doorway, the portals of which I cannot describe; but the door seemed to shut and shut all the time I was lingering over making a surrender. It seemed to shut almost to, and then I again promised the Lord, "I will". As soon as I said that a second time the door seemed to fly wide back and let a glorious light into the whole place . . . . When I saw that light, I fell flat on the floor; I could not face the light. While on the floor I had a warm heavenly feeling all over me from head to foot. I felt just as if a cloak was taken off my shoulders and a feeling of intense freedom came over me. I began to praise the Lord, and I have been praising him ever since. I lost in that moment my affliction of body and soul, but I did not realise how complete my bodily delivery had been until I got home.[15]

The following is a parallel case. Sister Florence Moss of Rayleigh, had been admitted to hospital, against her will, with a large tumour in her side. She had been a member of the Peculiar People for two years, and dreaded the prospect of the operation which the doctors had told her they would have to perform. On the Tuesday evening following her admittance to hospital:

a prayer meeting was held at Canning Town chapel at her request. Until this time she had suffered great pain in every part of her body; at about eight o'clock that evening she knew her brothers and sisters were in God's house, and wondered if they were praying for her; for the first time since the Thursday previous, she fell asleep and slept until just before six o'clock the next morning; she awoke without the slightest touch of pain, and all soreness had left her, which did not return at all. While the doctor made his examination of her that morning she saw his countenance change, and after some time he said to one of the nurses, "This is getting smaller" (meaning the tumour on her side). Throughout the day several doctors saw her, and all declared it certainly was smaller, though they all agreed it was a mystery. On the Thursday she was taken to a different ward, to see another specialist, but the doctors there ridiculed the idea of a tumour getting smaller, and said the other doctors must have made a mistake in the size of it. Just before five o'clock, when the last two doctors had left her, she felt she could endure no more; a violent fit of sobbing overcame her, she could not control herself at all. The nurse tried to quieten

her, but to no avail. This continued until she became exhausted;
after a time she glanced upward, and saw a strange form,
unearthly, all shining with a bright, beautiful light. A voice
spoke to her, which said, "Be not afraid, if they go too far, I
will come and take you Home." When this faded away it left
her calm and strengthened, and quite confident that the Lord
would not permit an operation. She was told another specialist
was coming to the Hospital to see her. Late in the morning, he
came and had a long conversation with some of the doctors,
and to her great joy, he settled all the reasoning and questioning
of the others with this conclusion, "Well, whatever was there,
there is nothing now." From this time she quickly gained
strength, and in two weeks and three days from the time of the
Prayer Meeting she was able to resume her ordinary
occupation.[16]

Many more cases and instances of healings could be added
to these to fuel either side of the argument. Let me conclude
this brief selection of cases, by quoting a letter sent to an
impartial investigator in 1907 from a devout family of Peculiars on Daws Heath: this expresses the *conviction* of healing
powers as plainly and powerfully as it is to be found
anywhere:-

Daws Heath, 11th March 1907.
Sir,
Seeing by the "Southend Standard" that you are of opinion that
these facts of faith healing ought to be known, I can give you
a brief outline of my experience. I am now 69 years old, and
my husband 70. We have neither of us had a doctor to us in our
lives, neither have we ever taken a dose of medicine. I have had
a family of children trusting in God, not in man. I have been
a Peculiar 49 years; I never gave one of my children a dose of
medicine nor applied any other means at any time, only faith
and prayer, according to God's Holy Word. We have had various afflictions, but the Powers of God have always been sufficient for us in every trouble. It is now about 40 years since the
Lord healed me of ague, instantly through the laying on of
hands in obedience to the Word of God. One of our children,
a boy, fell over a gate and fractured his collar bone, and for two
or three days he could not raise his hand in the least. Through
anointing with oil by an Elder and prayer, God healed the
child's arm immediately. One of our daughters, about fifteen
years old, had erysipelas in her head and face, and was blind a
day or two with it. Her face peeled five times, and then, through

faith and prayer, God healed her. Another, kicked by a horse when a lad – was healed in the same way. The same son, while in the Army, meeting with another accident, the bone in the head became injured and decayed. He was attended by a medical man, but to no effect; he then spent £15 on doctors, but all failed. He got in such a weak state of body that all hope of recovery was past, death appeared to have got hold of him. We then sent for one of the Elders of the Peculiar People, who laid hands on him and earnestly prayed in faith to our Great and Good God, Who heard and answered the prayer, and he began to get better from that time and now he is living here on the Heath healthy and well, and has in his possession between 20 and 30 pieces of bone which came out of his head. These are facts, and we are living witnesses. I can tell you many more deliverances God has wrought for us if required – these are only a few. Sir, you can make what use you like of this; we are not ashamed to testify to God's goodness anywhere. These are not things we have read out of a book, or done in a foreign land, but at Daws Heath, Thundersley.

Yours sincerely
G and E. THORINGTON.

P.S. These are things done only for the body, but I can tell you what God has done for my soul (if required). That is far more important than the body[17].

But no account of healing among the Peculiar People can be left at this point. There is another side to the picture: the following typical report may help to put it into perspective:

An inquest was held at West Ham yesterday on Rosina Benton, 70, widow of a former Elder of the Peculiar People. She had suffered from a hammer toe, and insisted on attending to it herself. Even when gangrene set in, she refused to have a doctor. She became unconscious on Saturday, and mortification arose and spread. She died from cardiac failure following exhaustion. In recording a verdict to this effect, the coroner remarked that the deceased, being of sound mind, could do as she liked regarding the calling in of a doctor[18].

The Peculiar People could not understand by divine healing, a power to assist the medical profession. For them, if faith meant anything it must be their all-in-all. If prayer and anointing with oil and the laying-on of hands could not heal the sick, they would not then take the sufferer to the doctor: they accepted the disease as being imposed by the will of

God, and to be borne according to his sovereign will. Some
no doubt regarded some sicknesses as God's means of cor-
rection; and certainly the breaking of bones was at one time
interpreted in this light[19]. Even if the sufferer appeared
entirely innocent and sinless, God in His wisdom could not
be mistaken; in the case of a child falling ill, the parents
might well reason that this was a punishment directed at
them, for their being too fond of the child, and neglecting
to praise God. Whatever the reason, they did not consider
it their right to interfere in God's inscrutable purpose – and
much less the right of any doctor or others not of the faith.
The patient would be tenderly cared for, and it would be
prayed over, but no doctor would ever come near the sick
bed.

The civil authorities viewed this sturdy resignation with
alarm and indignation, and were not slow to act. In the case
of adult members of the sect falling ill and refusing attention,
they were helpless, but when small children were allowed to
die, they stepped in and took the parents to court. (Indeed,
there does seem to be an anomaly in a religion that refuses
to allow its children to be baptised until they are committed,
but believes they can be healed by the faith of the parents
even before they are conscious.) (But see page 81 above.)

In the early days, the parents in these cases were usually
acquitted, proof that the same disease could be cured by
medical means being lacking. But as medicine grew into a
more exact science, and doctors began to assume through
their drugs and pills an almost divine infallibility, the number
of convictions grew. The extent of the punishments then
meted out to erring Peculiars, naturally varied in every case,
but the impression is that these too became harsher with the
passing years. To take a few examples at random:- Brother
William Rush of Tillingham: sentenced to one month's
imprisonment for failing to summon a doctor to his sick
child, although, in the event, the child recovered (1887).
Brother William Barnes and his wife Mary, convicted of
causing unnecessary suffering to their child, Lois Mary, 16,
who died of rheumatic fever while out in service: ordered to
pay a fine of £5 each (1900). Brother William Clark and his
wife Jane of Grays, charged with the manslaughter of their
daughter Emily, 6, who died from diphtheria: Brother Clark

sentenced to one month in prison without hard labour; his wife acquitted (the Elder of their church, Herbert Carter was sentenced to two months in prison without hard labour for advising the father not to call in the doctor, and for using his endeavours to prevent him doing so) (1907). Brother Thomas Whale of Wakering and his wife Charlotte, charged with the manslaughter of their son David, 7, who died of diphtheria: the father sentenced to two months' imprisonment, the mother again acquitted (1907). Brother George Horsnell of Canning Town and his wife, each sentenced to three months' imprisonment with hard labour for the manslaughter of their child Phyllis, 4, who died from measles followed by bronchitis (1909)[20]. Brother Henry Purkiss, sentenced to six months' imprisonment with hard labour, for the manslaughter of a child who died from diphtheria (1924). After this, cases grew more infrequent: the very last was heard in 1935, when Brother Thomas Levett of Stanford-le-Hope and his wife, were similarly charged with manslaughter, and acquitted.

The sadly numerous trials of Peculiars on these charges attracted wide attention: in particular, the contrast between the repellent charge of "criminal neglect", and the obvious integrity and loving affection of the bereaved parents, was often drawn, and every conviction aroused fresh controversy. George Bernard Shaw, of all people, interested himself in the matter, from a distance: in 1911 he wrote, repeating an argument often advanced:

> The calling in of the doctor is now compulsory except in cases where the patient is an adult and not too ill to decide the steps to be taken. We are subject to prosecution for manslaughter or for criminal neglect if the patient dies without the consolations of the medical profession. This menace is kept before the public by the Peculiar People. The Peculiars, as they are called, have gained their name by believing that the Bible is infallible, and taking their belief quite seriously . . . When I was a young man, the Peculiars were usually acquitted . . . Today all is changed . . . A modern doctor thinks nothing of signing the death certificate of one of his own diphtheria patients, and then going into the witness box and swearing a Peculiar into prison for six months by assuring the jury, on oath, that if the prisoner's child, dead of diphtheria, had been placed under his treatment instead of that of St James, it would not have died. And he does

so not only with impunity, but with public applause, though
the logical course would be to prosecute him either for the
murder of his own patient, or for perjury in the case of St
James. Yet no barrister, apparently, dreams of asking for the
statistics of the relative case mortality in diphtheria among the
Peculiars and among the believers in doctors, on which alone
any valid opinion could be founded. The barrister is as super-
stitious as the doctor is infatuated; and the Peculiar goes unpitied
to his cell, though nothing whatever has been proved except
that his child died without the interference of a doctor as effec-
tually as any of the hundreds of children who die every day of
the same disease in the doctor's care[21].

Let us examine in more detail one of the cases quoted above,
that of Brother Whale, the horseman of Wakering. This is
altogether typical of the kind of tensions that existed between
the Peculiars and the authorities over this matter.

Thomas Whale was born in south-east Essex in 1859, and
had worked on the land since the age of seven. He had been
a member of the Peculiar People since 1887. When his eldest
daughter (Margaret) went to school, she had taught her
father how to read and write and count money. Mrs Whale
usually did all the family's correspondence.

In April 1907, the younger of their two sons, David, died
of diphtheria. An inquest was held at the Castle Inn, Little
Wakering, under the Divisional Coroner. After the jury had
viewed the body (through the window of Whale's cottage,
as there was no mortuary in the district), Mr Whale was put
upon oath, and made a statement:

> My name is Thomas John Whale and I live at Little Wakering
> in the Wick Cottages. The deceased's name is David, and I don't
> think it has any other name. I am a labourer and work for
> Messrs P. Bentall at the Wick Farm. The deceased child is mine
> and is seven years of age – last September, I believe. He was a
> strong healthy child. He first commenced to ail last Friday
> week. He was in the field with me during the day and at
> eventime he complained that his head ached a little. It was a
> little hot, sir. We had been at the Half Way House (Farm) on
> the marshes during the day. On Saturday morning he got up
> as usual and had a little to partake of; but not as much as
> generally. He was about the house as usual all day and when he
> went to bed on the night he did not get up again. I went to Dr

Williamson, or rather I sent him a note on Monday morning.
I sent to him because I believed it was a case of diphtheria, sir.
Coroner asked why he sent for a doctor?
"Because I was advised by the Council and by my brethren that
I should report all cases of infectious disease: therefore I sent for
Dr Williamson."
Coroner: "But not with a view to have the child medically
treated, I suppose?"
– No, sir.
"You are a member of the Peculiar People, are you not?"
" – Yes, sir."
"Of the Original Peculiars?"
" – I don't know what they are."
"Some call themselves Original and some Liberty members:
what are you?"
A Juror: "An Elder of the Peculiars."
Whale: "No, not that, sir: a Help, sir."
The Coroner: "What is that? I don't understand that. When did
the doctor see the child?"
" – I sent him word to come and see the child."
"Were you present when he came to see the child?"
" – No, sir, but my wife was. I have her words if you want
them."
"Did you see the doctor at all?"
" – Not till after the child died at 4.10 a.m. on the 4th inst."
"Without having received any medical attention?"
" – Yes, sir; I can tell you what he said when he came to see
it."
The Coroner ruled this was not evidence: "You saw the child
daily?"
" – I helped to nurse it. What I did Dr. Williamson said was the
best. I gave it milk, which he said was the best, and mutton
broth, which was the best if he could take of it."
Coroner "He was not able to take either?"
" – He could not take it, sir. A little weak brandy and water
was given, but he could not take much because of the throat
being so sore. I was present and gave it to the child myself."
Coroner: "Brandy is a sort of medicine, isn't it?"
" – I don't think so, sir."[22]

It then emerged that another child of the Whales's had died
at the cottage just previous to the boy; she was his younger
daughter Ruth, a girl of sixteen and a half, who had come
home out of domestic service, suspected to have been suffering from consumption: she was buried on the day that the

boy had died. (The older daughter Margaret was married and lived away.) Upon this the inquest was adjourned.

When it reopened, there was a further development:

> *Coroner* (to Whale): "It is a fact that since we were here on Saturday last, another of your children has been attacked with diphtheria?"
>
> " – Yes, in a very mild form, sir".
>
> *Coroner*: "Anyhow, it is a fact that the child has been removed to the hospital and with your consent?"
>
> " – I did not say "Yes" or "No", sir."
>
> *Coroner*: "I believe you had it removed on the advice of Dr Williamson?"
>
> " – Yes, sir, but it went against me to do so[23]."

This was the elder of the Whale boys: Elijah, a boy of nine. He had been removed to the Isolation Hospital at Sutton nearby, where he was given anti-toxine treatment. He recovered to full health: indeed, he is alive today.

Mrs Charlotte Whale, the mother, who was a little deaf, was now questioned briefly.

> *Coroner* (to Mrs Whale): "The child (David) died on the Thursday morning?"
>
> " – Yes, sir."
>
> "Without having received any medical treatment?"
>
> " – Yes."
>
> "Didn't you think the child was dangerously ill?"
>
> " – Well, sir, I thought the Lord would take (*sic*); I thought it was the Lord's will He would take him from the time he was taken bad first.
>
> *Coroner*: You considered he was dangerously ill from the first?
>
> " – Yes, I knew and thought the Lord would take it."
>
> *Coroner*: "It is to be hoped you'll think differently some day."

The Coroner now turned to Dr Walter Cardy-Bluck, who had made the post mortem on the dead child:

> *Coroner*: "Do you think, from your examination, and what you found, that the child, being a healthy child, with the present day treatment of anti-toxine, would have had a chance of recovery?"
>
> *Bluck*: "Certainly, if it had been treated with anti-toxine in the first four days."
>
> *Coroner*: Can you tell us what your experience is as to the average results of the treatment?

Bluck: I had one death in the last 70 cases, and before the use of the treatment, when I saw the patient early, there used to be a death rate of 15 per cent only. I had 70 cases in the last five years, and the case which died I did not see until five days after the illness was contracted, when the disease was moribund.
Mr Whale: Did you ask the power of the living God?
Coroner: We can't go into that; that has no bearing on the case.
Mr Whale: God's power is higher than any man's. His breath is in our nostrils."

Dr Cardy-Bluck proceeded to detail the results of his post mortem. Dr Williamson was questioned next.

Coroner: "When you saw the child alive on the 8th, did you consider the case one of any great severity?"
" – Not at the time."
"Did you consider it was in its initial stage?"
" – I should say the child had been a day or two ill."
"The disease did not appear at that time to be severe?"
" – Not at that time: it was quite amenable to treatment."
"I believe you didn't offer to attend the child?"
" – No; because I knew in a previous case they would not let me nor have any treatment."
"That was when they had sent for you to see their girl Ruth?
". – They told me they belonged to the Peculiar People and did not believe in medical treatment."
"They would not allow you to treat the girl Ruth?"
" – No."

Although he had not offered to treat the child, he had recommended the foods and liquids to be given to it: milk, broth, beef tea and brandy.

Dr Grayson, Medical Officer of Health for Rochford Rural District, next took the stand. He had seen the child on Wednesday week at five in the evening. It was then in a desperate condition.

Coroner: "Did you see the father of the child?"
" – I did."
Coroner: "And did you advise him to have the child medically treated?"
" – I did, and to have it removed to the hospital."
Coroner: "He refused?"
" – He did."
Coroner: "Did he say anything?"

" – As near as possible, he said he put his trust in the Bible and in the Lord, and the help of man was but vain."

Coroner: "Did you tell him that the deceased could be treated by injection?"

" – I did, and that the treatment was much more successful now than it used to be formerly."

Coroner: "He still declined to allow the child to be removed and treated?"

" – He said the child would die there and he would rather it died at home."

Coroner: "Did you tell him he would be responsible if the child died?"

" – Yes, I told him I should have to hold him responsible, to which he said, "I suppose I must stand to it"."

Dr Grayson went on to say that there was no way that the child could have been removed from the care of the parents against their consent, without a magistrate's order, and that would have taken a day to obtain, and the child was in a serious condition.

A sanitary inspector who had also called at the house, and left disinfectants, was next questioned, and then Whale's employer, Mrs. Frances Harriet Bentall, who had met and talked with Whale over the child.

Mr Green, a Juror: "You consider him a good father?"

– "I think he is an excellent father, but for his mistaken ideas."

Coroner intervened and said he thought it was a generally accepted fact that this was so, and that the Peculiar People were excellent in every respect but for these ideas.

Mr. Green: "As to the question that this is a dairy farm. You say Whale is your head horsekeeper, and he would have nothing to do with the cows whatsoever?"

Mrs. Bentall: "That is so; as soon as I heard this he was kept away from them, and the man who attended the calves was taken away from his work."

All the evidence had now been taken: the Coroner summed up, and the Jury retired. For over an hour they were engaged in deliberation over their verdict, three times calling in the Coroner for advice. At length, in the afternoon, a verdict was agreed: "That the child David died of diphtheria and that there was wilful neglect on the part of the parents in not calling in a doctor." Both parents were therefore arrested, conveyed to Southend in a trap under the

Sister Gunn: the picture clearly shows the typical Peculiars' dress

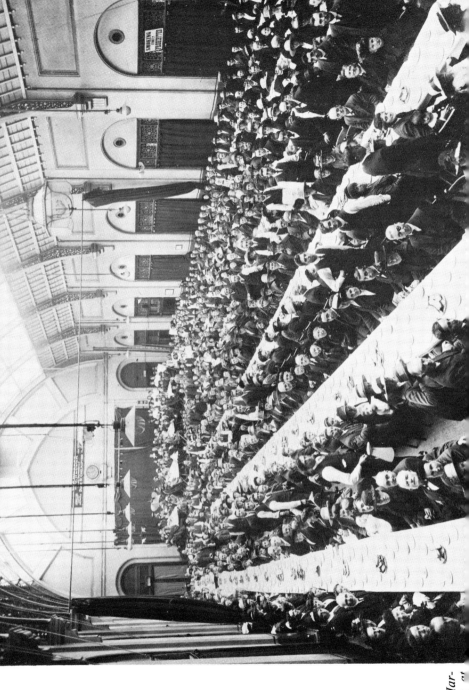

Tea is served at a Har-
vest Thanksgiving at

charge of a constable, accompanied by an inspector from the
N.S.P.C.C., and brought before the Mayor and charged.
Mrs Whale said the evidence was wrong: they had not
neglected their child. The charge was examined by the magistrates at Rochford the following Thursday. There, defence
urged that neither of the parents should be committed for
trial, and especially not Mrs. Whale, for the legal responsibility for the child rested with the father; also, it was he and
not she who had been given the advice that the child should
be treated with anti-toxine and removed to hospital. The
Bench accordingly dismissed the case against Mrs Whale,
but not that against her husband, who was now committed
for trial at the Summer Assizes in Chelmsford in June. Meanwhile, the health inspectors descended upon the Whales's
cottage: the house was pulled to pieces, their beds burned,
and all sorts of scorn was heaped upon them.

A few days after the magistrates' decision was taken, the
Peculiar People at Rochford held their anniversary services
at the Corn Exchange in that town, and Mr Whale addressed
a crowded evening meeting. His heart was full, and knowing
that here, at least, he would find the support of friends, he
gave expression to his emotions, and tried to explain the
convictions that had led to this prosecution. He praised God
for His goodness to him. Twenty years before, when he had
joined the People, he could hardly repeat the alphabet
through, but he felt thankful that since that day he had been
in a good school where he had learned and praised God. The
Spirit of God had taught him when he had read His Book
("Amen", "Bless God"). He did not deny that he had had
his troubles.

> Soon after he started to serve the God of Love, He caused a
> little affliction to fall on him, but he felt thankful that, by falling
> on his knees and talking to Him on the matter, God stopped it
> ("Praise Him", "Amen") . . . Thus he had proved the goodness
> and the love of God toward him in the pilgrim's journey
> ("Amen"). Last summer his dear wife was brought into great
> weakness and sore affliction, and the pain was so bad that it
> caused two of them to hold her down. Life seemed almost gone,
> but God, in answer to their prayers, delivered her ("Praise
> God", "Bless Him", "Amen"). Thus he had proved the good-
> ness and the love of God. Many said there was nothing in it,
> but he said there was a lot in it. ("Yes, brother", "Amen"). He

felt thankful tonight that the one who went first (Ruth) told
him she was about to go Home.

Speaking with great emotion, Brother Whale continued:

> She told me on her dying bed: "Father, don't cry; mother, don't
> cry. Lord Thy will be done" ("Amen, "Praise God"). She said
> moreover: "Don't look in the grave. I think, father, you had
> no rest last night, but you can rest tonight. I shall be at rest and
> you can rest" ("Praise God", "Amen").

He said further:

> He had felt through his little trial that it was not the trial he had
> to meet, but it was the Lord ("Amen"). He felt tonight that
> those who were gone were better off ("Yes". "Praise God").
> Twelve and a half hours after his first one died there was another
> taken ill (David), and he fell on his bed and felt "Lord, what is
> this you are bringing on me?" They would know hereafter. He
> felt God knew all what it was . . . He felt God would help him
> on, although he had had as much as he had been able to stand.

Speaking again at a very high pitch of emotion, Brother
Whale said:

> I hope my young friends, that our trials will not be any hin-
> drance to you young men and women, but I hope you will take
> courage and don't let our trial be any hindrance to you in the
> service of God ("No!", "Bless Him").

With the Bible outstretched in his hand, Brother Whale
loudly asked:

> "Shall I be an hypocrite?" Back came a loud chorus: "No,
> brother, stand firm. Praise God!" Again the speaker asked:
> "Shall I be an hypocrite?" "No brother", again came back the
> loud response. "No" shouted the speaker, now worked up to
> a pitch of great excitement, "No; not after I have proved His
> blessed Word. Shall I be an hypocrite? Oh no, I hope I shall
> not, because I believe it will be well in the end.

Three hours and many speeches and hymns later, the service ended; but on the station platform at night, where many
caught the last train home, the Peculiars were continually
bursting into hymns, and their singing could be heard all
over Rochford.

In June, Brother Whale stood in the dock in Chelmsford,
and when the charge was put to him, replied in a firm strong

tone: "Not Guilty, sir; I love my children too well for that, thank God". Clasping his hands, he surveyed the Court with a smile on his face, and later in the proceedings drew a red-edged Bible from his side pocket, and appeared to be studying it intently. The trial ran its inevitable course and the inevitable conclusion was reached. At length the time came for the Judge, Mr. Justice Phillimore, to sum up.

> In summing up, the Judge said that nobody sympathised more than he did with people who had conscientious convictions, but at the same time there were rules of civilised law and civilised society – well-accepted rules of health and life – that, whatever people might do with themselves, they must not play pranks with children who were under their charge. The Jury found the prisoner guilty of neglecting the child in a manner likely to cause unnecessary suffering or injury to health, and recommended him to mercy. The Judge deferred sentence until Monday, and said if the prisoner felt minded to send him a statement as to his future conduct, he would take it into consideration.[25]

When the prisoner was again brought up on Monday, the Judge said he was disappointed at not having received a statement in writing from him.

> "Have you sent any statement?" he asked.
> *Prisoner*: "I haven't sir, but I can say a few words."
> *The Judge*: "I don't wish you to say anything. What I explained to your counsel was that if I had reason to think that this sort of thing would not happen again, I would deal with you leniently."
> *Prisoner*: "I can't go against my own conscience."
> *The Judge*: "I know you can't. But I thought you had thought better about this matter. I don't pretend to understand all about your society, but I am told that there is a Liberty Section, which is ready to allow the members to call in medical aid."
> *Prisoner*: "That section has departed from us."
> *The Judge*: "Are you prepared to go with that Section?"
> *Prisoner*: "No, sir."
> *The Judge*: "Then you must come up for judgement tomorrow morning."

On Tuesday, the Judge said he had given the case very careful consideration, and he had come to the conclusion that the prisoner must have some punishment for allowing his child to suffer. He continued:

It is no use attempting to argue with you, nor is it my business. I quite understand that you are a man of good character and moral life, and I am glad that you have had the Jury's recommendation to mercy. I quite agree with that, and I can best express my own view by saying that it is not because you are wicked, but rather because you are silly and unreasonable, that I have decided for the sake of the children of this country to show that the law does not allow this thing to pass unnoticed. At the last Assize my brother Ridley passed sentence of one month in the second division on a member of your sect (Brother William Clark). As that has not been a sufficient deterrent, I am going to increase it, and it must be understood that it will be the duty of the Judges to increase the sentence from time to time until this matter is stopped. You must go to prison in the second division for two months.

Whale received the sentence with his hands clasped in prayer. Again, as he was taken from the dock, he smiled across the court to fellow brethren, and going down the steps to the cells he was heard to murmur: "All for Jesus!"

Two months later, a great crowd of Peculiars travelled up to Chelmsford from Southend, and gathered across the way from the Springfield Jail, where he had been incarcerated, waiting to greet him. Brother Whale was the first of a batch of prisoners to be released: as he appeared through the great gates of the prison, a shout of welcome went up. His wife and elder daughter rushed forward and embraced him with tears of joy, and the others pressed forward to shake him by the hand. Someone started singing the hymn, "Here's a welcome home", which all took up and rendered lustily. Then Brother George Anderson of Barking addressed the company, comparing the prosecutions of the Peculiar People to the persecutions of the early Christian church, with appropriate reference to their latest martyr. More hymns were vehemently sung, and finally "Onward Christian Soldiers" was taken up with such force and effect that an official stepped out from the prison entrance and angrily told them (according to one who was there) to "Make haste to get out of there!" and then they stopped. Brother Whale was taken into Chelmsford, given a good meal at a restaurant, and returned to Southend in triumph, in a motor-car.

His old job on the Wick farm was waiting for him. When he asked his employer Mrs Bentall: "What would you have

said had I given way?" her reply was: "I would never have
trusted your word again." So he continued on the farm until
1915, when he and his wife moved to a neighbouring village.
He became an Elder of the Wakering church; and both
remained firm Peculiars right to the very end of their lives.
Mrs Whale died in 1936, aged 73; and Brother Whale, aged
79, in 1938; by which time – strange though it is to think –
the era of the pure and awesome faith of the Peculiar People
had already passed away for ever.

CHAPTER VI

Thoughts on The Past
and The Present

I esteem it a privilege to have taken some part in the research
necessary for the compiling of this historical record. It is
with a deep sense of loyalty to the memory of the men and
women of my early years that I avail myself of the· opportunity to write the concluding chapter.

Firstly then I write in retrospect, as my association began
at the beginning of this twentieth century. Secondly I will
endeavour to give a brief appraisal of their present standing
as "The Union of Evangelical Churches".

One is very conscious that the written word can only
inadequately convey the deep spiritual quality of the lives of
the people referred to. One had to live with them to really
know their worth. Memories that come to mind bring with
them happy recollections of the Annual Summer Outings
and Winter Anniversary Services, or "Treats" as they were
then called; also, later, the outstanding meetings and united
gatherings marked by so many conversions and manifestations of Divine Healing. To have had some share in these
experiences is something never to be forgotten. One's only
regrets are some of the dark shadows of the earlier years,
though happily, by the first part of the century, they were
passing into the realm of history.

However, owing so much to those who stood firm
through every trial and persecution, one feels these people
should not be forgotten but revered for their faithfulness and
integrity. If the thoughts outlined in this concluding chapter
bring into greater relief the honesty of purpose and dedica-
tion of those referred to, if someone's faith and trust in their

God should be stimulated through the reading, the purpose in writing will have been achieved.

Banyard's Day

It is a far cry back to the days when James Banyard, the founder of the Peculiar People, could have been seen with a few of his humble followers wending their way through the leafy lanes, or the open roads of the corn-growing district of the Essex countryside. Here was a man with a mission, journeying to the neighbouring villages surrounding his home town of Rochford, proclaiming to all who would hear him the glorious news of a personal salvation, the doctrine of the "New Birth" and consequent ability to conform to "Holy Living". As we have read in the foregoing chapters, the listeners that would gather round him were in the main of the labouring classes, frequently of agricultural stock, often illiterate and unlearned. Who was to know then of the great impact this fearless preacher of the Gospel was to make on the County of Essex? J. H. Burrows in his *Historical Notes of Southend-on-Sea* (1909), makes this point:

> Banyard's teaching had a marked influence on the agricultural population, and during the last fifty years it may be said to have entirely changed the thought and habits of hundreds of men and women of South Essex.

Another observer comments:

> From the commencement, the blessing of God seems to have attended their preachings, rough lives have been softened, and bad ones purified.

In simple terms, following the great change that he experienced when truly "born again" and infilled with the Holy Spirit (as recorded in the initial chapters of this book), Banyard could not keep this great personal experience to himself; his burden was that others too might know the joys of personal salvation through faith in Jesus Christ, that they too might know a power that could lift the fallen, and bring life and cheer into the drab lives endured by so many of the working classes of this day.

As his converts entered into this new experience of sins

forgiven, this deliverance from mere formalism – or in some
cases from crime and degradation – so distinct was the
change that it was observable to all. The Word of God
became not only their charter for Holy Living, but also, not
infrequently, their education in a literal sense for, deploring
their illiteracy, by patient and prayerful study, with the
assistance sometimes of their own children, they were eventually able to read for themselves certain basic truths of God's
Word.

"Enoch walked with God"

It was through Bridges that Banyard came to see constant
fellowship with God as the glorious privilege of all truly
born-again believers. Bridges had accepted it through the
preaching of Robert Aitken, as mentioned on p. 16: This
truth of "daily walking and talking with God" Banyard
embraced in its entirety, and from this his spiritual strength,
and that of his followers, ensued. Preposterous, some might
think; but the results that followed proved his convictions
well-founded.

To Banyard this was basic; it predominated over everything else. His concern to hear God's voice and be led by it,
believing that as each new day unfolded, He would reveal
His will for them and meet all their circumstances, is borne
out by Banyard's preliminary instructions to the Church to
seek God's face in prayer at 5 am daily, deeming this more
paramount than any set of rules. Dispersing from these early
gatherings they jealously guarded this attitude of mind, this
consecration of purpose, this great desire that nothing should
break or mar, this vital communion, until they would have
opportunity to meet together again for corporate worship.

This attitude of "walking and talking with God" produced
many of the characteristics recorded in this book. In a few
years they became a distinct body of believers. The name
they eventually assumed, "The Peculiar People" (or, as they
would sometimes style themselves, "The People of God"),
seemed utterly appropriate. Taken in its Scriptural rendering,
it suited a people who in speech were so careful as to be
easily distinguishable, who were so sober in manner yet in
countenance so cheerful, who in circumstances were so poor

yet so willing to share, whose dress was so singular yet so
neat and plain – all resulting from this careful walk with
God. No finery, no display or pride, nor anything that might
endanger this vital personal standing with God, was counte-
nanced: they called it "living to God". No wonder these
people were such a force!

A Nottingham correspondent wrote to Mark Sorrell:

> For one generation they were in the centre of the Creator's plan,
> way in front of any other denomination for 50 years.

Why for only half a century? Do we assume that from then
onwards there was an abatement of this holy zeal, a gradual
decline?

The Changing Scene

The words "changing scene" are used here advisedly.
Although readers' opinions may be divided as to what con-
stitutes progress or decline in spiritual matters, it is evident
that we must admit to at least some of the changes and their
effects.

First, we refer to the source of their strength: daily communion with God, observed by congregation and leaders
alike, a devout and praying people utterly dependent on
God. Could this be undermined? If so, it would halt and
eventually reverse the trend. Since the Fall in Eden, where
intimate communion between God and man was the norm,
the great enemy of souls has concentrated his strongest influences to this end.

The foregoing chapters reveal a series of inner conflicts
within a community which had commenced so well as to be
almost identical to the New Testament Church. But the
doctrinal differences which arose, and the contention surrounding them, seemed sometimes far removed from the
attitudes of daily communion with God. The miracle is that
they survived at all. Surely God had a purpose for them, and
one is convinced that God had His hand upon this people,
just as he did on the Early Church, with all its problems and
complexities.

An early independent observer and reporter expressed
sympathy and amazement:

Of persecutions they have had more than enough, but have survived the ordeal, and as for internal strife, it has been and is sharp and bitter, but they still stand.

No longer was the fiery 19th century preacher Banyard to be seen in the market square; no longer on a still summer's evening could the voice of Thomas Rayner preaching the Gospel in the High Street of Great Wakering he heard as far afield as Barling Magna. Certainly there were those who still retained much fire and zeal, but in general the people were moving over to the defensive: the zealous open-air preaching against the kingdom of darkness was waning somewhat.

Changes through Legislation

The latter part of the nineteenth century saw the beginnings of many social reforms and the corresponding legislation to enforce them. Curiously this people, so honest in their dealings, so desirous to do the right thing at all times, were adversely affected by some of these laws, which bore heavily upon their spiritual ideal of complete trust in God, irrespective of man.

Some changes were sudden; others, although slow, influenced their lives no less surely. The village scene was changing. No longer would the "sister" midwife be seen leaving a cottage in the small hours of the morning. In the evening, the Elder appeared less frequently on his mission to visit the sick. The anomalies of "progress" and legislation were being felt. Sturdily and courageously the people resisted what affected their beliefs, prepared on this account to suffer imprisonment at times rather than yield. The preceding chapters show that rightly or wrongly this developed into a losing confrontation with secular authority. They had no choice but to concede to more liberal views or else remain indefinitely at variance with the law.

In spite of all this, the work progressed. Conversions were frequent, signs followed their preaching, and numerous are the written testimonies of Divine Healing, with hundreds more not recorded. If the laws of the land must be obeyed, they were prepared to concede only the minimum when it encroached upon that important tenet of their faith, complete trust in God.

But the mighty arm of the law had little time for what it regarded as mere religious scruples: reforms for the country as a whole had come to stay. Strange as it may appear to us today, these very worthy measures to benefit the working classes (the National Insurance Act of 1911, also in later years the notion of a Welfare State and apparent affluence attending it), somehow seemed alien to the simple faith and trust in Providence which the Peculiars wished to perpetuate. But the march of "progress" accelerated in succeeding years, and could not be halted. Ironical as it may appear, although they shared in its benefits, their principles were threatened by it. Increasingly, their attitude was one of conciliation and compromise, rather than confrontation.

Twentieth Century Influences

We have seen that persecution could not destroy them but rather urged them to greater earnestness, strengthening the bond of unity between them. But more subtle influences were already at work. Many times had they prayed that "the great wheel of Providence might turn in their favour", not only for themselves but, to use a term familiar to them, "for the poor at large". Slowly but surely the social reforms in the later half of the Victorian Era brought this about. By the beginning of the 20th century it could truly be said that the praying mother would no longer have to be on her knees asking for daily bread for her hungry children, or for clothing in which to send them to school. Always a thankful people, they were quick to praise God for the blessings they appreciated. But Christian history, and the records of the Peculiar People, show that an increase in material prosperity is not conducive to greater spirituality.

Almost imperceptibly the pioneering zeal for which they were so marked, began to lose its edge. A visit to any one of their meeting places would have shown no marked visible change. They still held tenaciously to their mode of worship. They were men and women who during the week commanded respect as loyal servants. Some had become masters, some skilful tradesmen, some shopkeepers, and others tenant farmers. At the testimony meeting on any Sunday morning, individual praise and thankfulness was still the predominant

feature of the service. True, they were better dressed, but
there they sat, the brothers and sisters, on alternate sides as
usual. Admittedly, the bonnet was less conspicuous on the
sisters's side, but the brothers with their clean-shaven faces
had changed little. During the meeting the sick could still be
seen going forward for anointing with oil and laying on of
hands by the Elders, according to the scriptural instruction.
They were "settling down"; active persecution was ceasing;
so many difficulties had been overcome; they were a happy
spiritual "family" with better meeting-places and established
Sunday Schools for their children. The healing of wounds
and the great re-union added to their sense of joy, satisfaction
and well-being.

Not only were the bonds of spiritual unity now restored,
but they were now bound together by a legal Trust Deed:
they had become a denomination.

But changes of a dramatic nature, not only for them but
for every man, woman and child in the land were only just
around the corner: from peace and stability to war declared,
August 1914. We read the experiences of men imprisoned
for their faith with sadness, mixed with admiration for their
courage and steadfastness. Everywhere Christendom was
being shaken. Would things ever be the same again? Every
facet of the Christian faith was affected; no denomination
escaped the impact of those frightful years. Nor would the
Peculiar People ever be quite the same again.

The questions which were arising in the thoughts and
minds of the younger generation demanded to be answered.
To the credit of the Elders and Council of the People, they
for the most part did all they could to consolidate the community again, but some young people who now had wider
horizons, were now unsettled. This led, not to "secession"
but to a gradual loss of individuals to more liberal
denominations.

What was to be done? There were many hours of discussion and deliberation in Council; Council minutes record the
rigidness of some Elders, the compassion and tolerance of
others.

The simplicity of worship which had so strongly appealed
to them as a working-class community was being chal-
lenged, and some of its winsomeness was fading. This was

almost inevitable: this was the backlash of the tragedy of the
War and its effects in general. What of the congregations,
the brothers and sisters? Undeniably, some entrenched themselves more firmly than ever in their traditional practices,
honestly believing that at all costs they must safeguard "The
truth", not realising perhaps what was obvious to some of
the leaders: that no community can stand still, however
firmly it may entrench itself, without eventually declining.

Some caught the vision of the new post-War society
around them, a society of disillusioned men and women
with new needs. Never was evangelism needed more. Great
efforts were put into local mission programmes and some
new "causes" were established. Greater freedom was allowed
for youthful participation. Generally, a more outward-looking concept was evolving; perhaps too outward-looking for
some, but dramatic changes had come affecting the "family"
as a whole in a real way.

They were still a pious God-fearing people, but by this
time that fire and zeal which had once put them in the
forefront had further abated. They were not so different
from many other religious bodies, though no motion had
ever been passed in their Council rescinding or amending
any of their Doctrines and Beliefs: every new convert was
expected to abide by them. No: that which had been tested
and tried should be adhered to; no principle dare be given
up; with God's help they would work out their own salvation. But they were losing that magnetism which had once
drawn in the unconverted.

Yet another shattering blow was to fall. Perhaps the whole
social structure of the nation has never fully recovered from
the demoralising effects of World War Two, especially
through the evacuation and dispersal of family units. Once
again war took its toll within the community; some meeting
places were closed, never to be rebuilt or reopened; whole
families were evacuated and settled elsewhere.

A Momentous Step

It was a time for some hard thinking and prayerful consideration. Was there a future for the denomination? If so, how
and where? To remain so insular any longer seemed to spell

out eventual extinction, the quenching of the flame which had once burned so brightly.

It is not surprising that in 1956, the Council of Elders issued the following statement to be read by every member of the community:

THE NAME OF THE PECULIAR PEOPLE

Propositions: In the absence of any acceptable suggestion for a revised name, and in view of the majority vote already recorded:

THAT we lovingly urge our Churches as a body and our membership as individuals to abandon the name "The Peculiar People", and to accept as a new title for our community – THE UNION OF EVANGELICAL CHURCHES.

THAT for local description we suggest adding the term EVANGELICAL CHURCH to the name of town, village, locality or road in which our Chapel is situated, whichever may be deemed most suitable to the case.

THAT for legal or other official purposes, we denote our community as "THE UNION OF EVANGELICAL CHURCHES", formerly known as "The Peculiar People".

These considerations are based upon various considerations, including:-

(a) the name "The Peculiar People" is undoubtedly a barrier to our progress, particularly in town areas, and a hindrance to many outside the Church who might otherwise be brought under the sound of the Gospel and into Christian fellowship.
(b) The change of name would not of itself have any detrimental effect upon our doctrinal standard and Scriptural practices, or upon our fellowship or mode of worship, but would impress rather our adherence to the great evangelical doctrines of the Christian faith.

(c) The reasons for our original exclusiveness have long since ceased to be valid, with the scriptural awakening and increasing spiritual unity of many contemporary Churches.

(d) The increasing signs of the imminence of the Second Coming of our Lord and Saviour Jesus Christ, and the consequent brevity of our period of testimony, demand that we should without delay remove any and every obvious barrier to our service for Him.

(e) The steps recommended would not alone remove a hindering sectarian barrier, but would seem to be in harmony with the movement of the Holy Spirit, which has been noticeable for many years, drawing together in active fellowship (if not into organic unity) the Lord's people who cling to and desire to maintain the evangelical doctrines of the Christian faith.

N.B. The foregoing need not await or be dependent upon any association we may form with other Christian bodies. It is suggested as a step to "putting our own house in order".

What of today?

So the name, "The Peculiar People", which for well over a century had identified this zealous people, was relegated to the past. What of the future? Would the new generation, adopting this new title of "Union of Evangelical Churches", live up to the implications of this name as faithfully as their forebears did to theirs? Twenty years have now passed since this change of name. What criteria is it relevant to use in our endeavour to give a fair and unbiased assessment of their present standing? So much has changed. The distinctive marks of the Peculiar People are but a memory, though a precious one to some.

We have seen that the county of Essex is incalculably indebted to the "Banyardites": although the schisms and divisions of the early years are regrettable, the soundness of their preaching backed up by the quality of their lives, left behind indelible impressions. The march of time has had its effects, but the truths they preached remain. As for the present generation, let not the reader assume that there has been a deliberate departure from the faith of their fathers. Leaders and members of the Union of Evangelical Churches would be prepared to give assent to the bedrock truths of the Word of God, and many still avail themselves of the privileges of Divine Healing as revealed to the pioneers of this people.

If we pause for a moment to make a brief reappraisal of the relevant factors concerning their claims to be "Evangelical Churches", we see that slowly the predominant emphasis has moved from Divine Healing, which was so much in the forefront in former years, to the pressing needs of the task of Evangelism, especially amongst the up and coming generation. Of the twenty-five churches of the Union, the majority have thriving Sunday Schools, and a flourishing Youth work, which has its own Council (formed in 1962), working closely with the parent body – the UEC. This has a broad spectrum of activities, all geared to the spiritual growth of committed young people and outreach amongst others who are not so committed: this includes periodical Youth Rallies from all the churches of the Union, combined with sports activities in the summer months and meetings to promote and encourage Christian loyalties and to give instruction on the best methods of outreach. A very practical aspect of this work is the Tape Recording Department – an up-to-date method of presenting the claims of the Gospel, which by working closely with the Disabled Christian Fellowship has proved to be an inspiration to the less fortunate.

The association of the U.E.C. with the F.I.E.C., has strengthened the bonds of fellowship with like-minded Evangelical Christians, which is perhaps seen at its best at the Annual Conference and Houseparty held annually at Herne Bay, Kent, where spiritual refreshment is enjoyed together, and it is worthy of note that in recent years the bond of fellowship has been reaffirmed with the Sussex community bearing the name of the Dependants (the Cokelers). Their founder, John Sirgood, was inspired by the same zeal for souls as James Banyard of Rochford through coming into contact with the preacher William Bridges of London and hearing him expound the doctrine of the "New Birth". Both were greatly influenced by him but went their seperate ways to be used by God for the extension of His kingdom. Relations between the two communities have always been very cordial though separate in administration. It is good to know that recently a definite link has been made with these fellow believers, which should be for the profit of all concerned.

Enterprise has also been shown in that additional facilities in the form of auxiliary buildings have been added to most "causes" to meet the needs of the rising generation. Yet, although they have joined the mainstream of churches bear-

Above: *Sunday
School outing to West
Mersea, 1915*

Below: *Open-air
meeting in the square
at Tillingham, c. 1900*

Conscientious Objectors of the Peculiar People in Dartmoor, 1916

Back Row:

Walter Whybrew *(Witham, Southend)*	Arthur Sandford *(Tillingham, Prittlewell)*	Fred Gilmore *(Grays)*
Ernie Nunn *(Corringham)*	George Bocking *(Cressing)*	John Atkins *(Methodist Southchurch)*

Middle Row:

John Jarvis *(Rayleigh)*	Arthur Sutton *(Romford)*	Jonathan Hinton *(Daws Heath)*
Samuel Philby *(Canning Town)*	Charlie Hills *(Silvertown)*	

Front Row:

George Nunn *(Grays, Corringham)*	Walter Jarvis *(Rayleigh)*	Fred Outten *(Stanford)*
John Mackintosh* *(Canning Town)*	Ernest Hockley* *(Barking)*	Will Hammond* *(Ramsden Heath)*

*The surviving members of the group

ing an evangelical witness, it would be incorrect to say that they are "way out in front" today. Undoubtedly they still have a part to play in the great Church of Christ: the message of the Gospel is still faithfully preached, and sound doctrine adhered to. A visitor to any one of their meeting places would immediately sense a real warmth of Christian fellowship. What then: is the vitality of earlier days missing? Suppose it were possible to bring back the customs and habits of the people as seen in former years, that would not in itself be the answer. Some indeed would not be relevant today. No, it is on a deeper level.

Here I beg leave for a personal comment. I believe with all sincerity that there is only one answer to this vital question, which is relevant not only to the Union of Christian Churches but to all who claim to be the "Lord's People". What is lacking in our assemblies today is that dynamic power of the Holy Spirit as our forebears knew it. Banyard, like all men who have been used by God to revive His work, realised the dearth of this in the formal religious life he was living. Being an honest and sincere man, he was humble enough to acknowledge his need, hence his exclamation to Bridges: "I feel I have no worthwhile religion".

God's pattern never changes. We are reminded of the religious zealot, Saul of Tarsus who, when smitten down on the Damascus road, exclaimed: "Lord, what will you have me to do?" If we would share in any revival work again we must have a renewal of this power that has energised revival preachers such as the Wesleys, Whitefield, and later Banyard, through the course of the centuries. Remissness and lukewarmness we must acknowledge humbly, entreating: "Lord, what will you have us to do?" for our generation.

This book cannot fail to remind us of the value of the goodly heritage, of which we are the recipients. Thank God for the humble men who have shown us the way. No serious-minded reader, whether "born again" or otherwise, will remain unchallenged when turning its pages. The majority of the men and women who are referred to have entered into their rest, but their witness was not in vain. "They rest from their labours and their works do follow them". Only the spiritual harvest will reveal how extensive the effects and impact of this local revival have been. Beyond the population of Essex it has had far-reaching results: the "bread cast upon the waters" is being found "after many days" in this land and others too.

Frank Smith, retired U.E.C. Minister

Three Life Histories

I Isaac Anderson

Born Prittlewell, Essex, 1833.
Heard the Curate of Prittlewell preaching against Banyard, and Banyard's reply, 1848.
Joined the Brethren at Rochford, 1851.
Ordained an Elder at Maldon (at the same meeting as the four original Bishops were ordained), 1852.
Leading Elder at Southend until his death, 1910.

The following is taken from *The Life History of Isaac Anderson A Member of the Peculiar People* (Southend 1896).

I was born in North Street, Prittlewell, on August 4th, 1833. My father (James Anderson) was born in the Village, and had lived there all his life. There were ten of us in family – seven boys and three girls – of whom I was the sixth.

I was only five years of age when Queen Victoria was crowned, but I can just remember a dinner to celebrate the event being given in Milton Hall Meadow, where Park-road is now situated, to the people of Prittlewell, Southchurch, Southend, and Leigh. I had but little schooling and first went to the Free School, North-street, close to where the Old Pump stands; my parents paying a penny a week for each of us. At that time the boys from Southend used to attend the same school, as there was no such institution there. For a short time I went to a private school; where Samuel, Fred, and Henry Garon attended. I have often thought what a sufferer our master was; "Dictionary" Bradley, we used to call him, on account of the tremendous words he uttered to make us boys use. He suffered from a complaint known by us in those days as "Chalk gout;" and at times little balls of chalk came out of the joints of his fingers and toes. I have never seen the like since. Mr Firman, a gentleman who farmed some land where the Waterworks now stand, paid for my education at this school. Southend was small at that time; in fact, Mr Firman was the only farmer who supplied the town with milk. We were kept at school all the week excepting on Saturdays, and as a rule on that day my brothers and sisters and I used to walk to Southend beach to get sand to sprinkle on the floors of the house. We had no carpets. We enjoyed the walk. There were fields from the village to Whitegate – which until recently was known as Whitegate-road – and at the end of the fields there was a great white gate and from which the road derived its name. From the gate to the Thatched Cottage, which until recently stood at the corner of Cliff Town-road, there was a road with corn fields on either side; Mr. Price lived in that cottage for years.

To show the growth of Southend since that period, I might mention there were only seven buildings between that corner and the Pier. The British Schoolroom was one of the number, and was used by the "Independents" as a place of worship. There were no other churches or chapels in Southend. A Mr Clark kept the only grocer's shop up the Hill and Mr. Fox was the proprietor of the Post Office and grocery establishment down the Hill.

The old wooden pier was in course of construction during that time.

The village was stirred just before 1840 through an agitation which arose between the Vicar (Dr Nolan) and the parishioners – more especially the bellringers. The doctor was a very aged gentleman and for various reasons his parishioners were anxious to get rid of him. He moved against the bellringers and they, to spite him, effected an entrance to the belfry and began to ring the bells in the middle of the night. This enraged the old Vicar, more especially the breaking into the belfry, as he kept the keys; so, to save a repetition of the scandal, it is said he cut the ropes with a carving knife. Much unpleasantness followed; one man was sent to prison; a song was composed in the interval; but at length the old Vicar left the parish.

The winter of 1840 was very hard. My father was unable to do any work, and with four of us boys he was compelled to go into Rochford Union. Mother, with three of the little ones, stayed at home and were supported by several kind friends. We were in the Union nine weeks, but during that time I obtained most of my education. I was just over seven years of age when we came out, and soon after I went to work at Brick House farm for Mr E. Kilworth, with whom I stayed sixteen years. Mr. J. Heygate farmed part of the land – their farms adjoining. During these years I went down into the lowest and darkest valley that a young man ought to go: yet during the same period I felt raised to the highest, brightest mount any mortal could reach.

I commenced work feeding cattle, and the wage I received was one shilling a week. We did no more work on Sunday than we were obliged: and got all the work ready on Saturday. Mr. Heygate's farm joined ours and consequently I knew the family well – especially for their kindness. Sometimes their hens laid on Mr Kilworth's part of the farm and when we found the eggs we took them to the house, and every time we went the servants gave us a lump of bread and cheese, or meat. If we found several eggs we boys used to take care only to take them one at a time, so as to get the food more often. I continued to work for Mr. Kilworth, and as years went by my money increased, until at last I received man's pay – nine to twelve shillings per week; the wage varying according to the price wheat sold at; which was from £3 to £5 per quarter. I remember bread being one shilling a loaf, but that was before Free Trade and during the Crimean War.

Eventually I, with my father and two brothers, went threshing, and it was indeed hard work. I was a growing lad and was always hungry, as it were. My breakfast consisted of a mess of water and flour, but this was not enough to satisfy nature, and long before dinner time I felt so fatigued and hungered I could have eaten my fingers if it had been possible. I could scarcely walk home at the end of the day's work. The men used to call thrashing "swinging dismal" and my experience made me believe this was a true name for it; they were indeed hard times – never to be repeated in history, I hope.

I could not blame my parents in the least; they were very kind. I never heard my father use a foul expression in my

life. I could only wish they had each lived to enjoy and to
see the improvements I see. Still I have a good hope of seeing
them again. My father was so happy when he came to die
that my uncle said he wished he were in his place. My eyes
flow with tears when I think of them and what they endured;
yet they were content.

We labourers living in the country were in such darkness
and were so ignorant that we moved with our whole being
against Free Trade and the introduction of thrashing
machines and other implements now used. We were under
the impression they would take what living we had away
and we should be destitute.

Many times before this we had wondered and puzzled
ourselves as to where Mr Kilworth and the other masters
got their money from to pay us at the end of the week; we
were in such ignorance.

(It was at about this time, 1851, that Anderson began to
attend the meetings of the Banyardites at Rochford in earnest, and was persuaded that "it was the very same Saviour
in the spirit that came down on the day of Pentecost" that
they possessed, and which worked through them. Elsewhere, he describes his conversion to their religion in the
following terms.)
"I determined to join the Brethren. On February 17th 1851,
a special meeting was held at Rochford (to celebrate the
salvation of William Bridges). I set my mind on going and
went five miles; leaving my father at work on Southchurch
Hall Farm. I told him where I was going, but he made no
answer. As I was walking along the road I had a fearful
struggle with my feelings. I was tempted not to go and not
to carry out my purposes, but at length, after great battling
with myself, I reached the chapel and was baptised with
water by James Banyard and admitted into the Church and
recognised as a member. The following day I went to the
Hall Farm to work, and while busily engaged there came a
blessed power upon me which cleared away all my doubts
and assured me I was born again. I was satisfied it was the
Holy Spirit of God descending upon me to keep me from
sinning and to help me to please God, which hitherto I had
not been able to do. On Sunday I met with the friends at

Banyard's Chapel, Rochford, and it seemed to me as though
heaven had commenced below while praising God in the
highest. I was filled with joy unspeakable."

Not long after this the London, Tilbury, and Southend
Railway was opened (1856), and most of the young men left
Prittlewell, going into the towns. I was tired of my work
and gave Mr Kilworth a week's notice. It was not usual to
do so, but I did, having been with him such a long time. He
was astonished and said, "Where are you going, Isaac?" I
answered "I do not know: I can't stand this work any
longer." I left him and immediately went down Mill-Lane
– now Avenue-road – and fell down on my knees under a
bush and prayed to the Lord to guide me. I got up and
walked on. Just about that time the London, Tilbury, and
Southend Railway Company were carting the "slips" from
the Park Street bridge to Leigh, and a number of navvies
were engaged in the work. I went and asked for work, but
I had trouble in getting it; for the men, working in couples
on a truck, were loath to take me as a mate. Still, one of the
navvies, named Pavis, took me with him, and we loaded
our truck before the others; he doing part of my share. After
a while he went to chapel at Prittlewell with me.

Subsequently I went to work at Shoebury for Colonel
Gardiner [sic], as gardener. Colonel Gordon was said to be
a brother of General Gordon who went to Khartoum and
there lost his life. Many times Colonel Gardiner interested
me by telling me of the scenes through which he had passed
during his career. On one occasion he took me into his
parlour, and besides presenting me with a copy of Pilgrim's
Progress, which I have always prized, told me of the bitter
persecution the Jews had been subjected to in foreign coun-
tries – of persecutions which had come under his direct
notice. When I had finished his garden I continued to work
in the Garrison, employment being found for me in con-
structing pontoons for the officers, etc., to practise making
bridges over water. The old navvies knew I was a young
beginner, and many of them overloaded my barrow so that
in the wheeling it might turn over, but I got on all right,
excepting that the work drew blood from my hands, which
ran down between my fingers. I continued at this work for

some time, and when water was being laid on in the barracks
some time after, Mr J. W. Harris recommended me to the
plumbers, who engaged me to look after the fires and heat
the lead for them. This work was much easier, and together
with the "tips" and over-time my wages were double those
I received when "Swinging dismal". When the contract was
finished Mr Harris found me other employment and I got
on well under him and during that time married. I, of course,
then lived at Shoebury, and the walk to the Chapel at Prittlewell was very long. I used to go every Tuesday and
Thursday evenings, reaching there at seven. On Sunday
mornings the services commenced at six o'clock and I invariably missed the first ones. Many a winter's night I have
walked to Shoebury by the seaside between nine and eleven,
all alone; meeting no one except the Coastguards on their
beats. I remember one Sabbath morning it was so dark it
was impossible to keep to the path. I was walking along
enjoying my meditations when suddenly I found myself in
a hole of brambles on Shoebury Common. Fortunately, I
was able to get out without help, and having recovered
myself continue my journey; feeling more blessed than Bunyan when in Bedford Goal [sic]. After that I returned to
Prittlewell to make it my home, it being far more convenient
to walk to Shoebury to work than from Shoebury to Prittlewell to chapel and then return late at night.

Time went on and eventually I left Shoebury altogether,
and for six years Mr Jas. Tabor found me work at Earl's
Hall. This was not so remunerative. In the winter time I
thrashed oats at a shilling a quarter. One week I earned six
shillings and fourpence, and out of that I had to pay a man
to help me dress the oats, so I had not much left to take
home. I could not keep on at this work, finding it so hard
and not earning sufficient to support my family. Just at that
period the authorities commenced making up the roads in
Porters Town (Southend), and I was taken on road-making
again. Whilst engaged here I was included in the gang who
laid the first sewer in Southend. Things went on smoothly
for a time and I added to my income by tilling a piece of
land at Prittlewell.

Subsequently I joined a gang of men engaged by Mr J.
Brown in unloading barges, and still later, in the year 1872,

I started throwing down the banks round the Square Field
– now known as Warrior Square – for Mr Venables; Mr
Denison being the surveyor. Mr Waterhouse, the then Local
Board Surveyor, also connected with the Water Works
Company and agent for the New Town, was very useful in
supervising. After a while I was appointed foreman over
eleven men engaged on the Estate. We made the roads and
then planted the trees, over which I have had charge up to
the present. I first had trouble with gipsy people and excur-
sionists, but, with the aid of ex-Superintendent Hawtree, I
managed them all right without taking anyone to Court.

I have never slept from home more than four nights in
succession farther than Shoebury, and I do not remember
laying in bed one day through sickness. I have never been
called to a Court of Justice either as plaintiff, defendant, or
witness, and it has not cost me a penny for physic for myself,
wife, or family, and I do not owe a penny to any man.

My family have had more opportunites than I ever had
and are more suitable for business than I am. If I were out
of work today, I should seek work sweeping the roads and
be more satisfied in that occupation than any business. I have
always worked pleasantly with my masters and have not had
a single cross word with my present employer.

II John Hockley

Born Wickford, Essex, 1861
Joined the Peculiar People at Ramsden Heath, 1882:
Opened a chapel at South Green for preaching 1887 – 1893
*Served the Peculiar People thereafter at Southend, Chelmsford, Wick-
ford, Leigh etc. in missionary work.*
Died 1930

The following extracts are taken from a remarkable manuscript of some 40,000 words by John Hockley, entitled *The lifes story of John Hockley the Converted Bellringer* which was written in the early years of this century. The manuscript is in the possession of John Hockley's son, Mr Ernest Hockley, who has generously given me permission to quote from it. Spelling and punctuation are as in the original. (see photograph on p   ). These extracts, from the earlier part of the MS, describe the events leading up to Hockley's conversion (pps. 1–38).

I was born in the year 1861 on the 1st day of September in the Villiage of Wickford in Essex. at that time a bungalow was being built for my parents at Wickford Wick. at that farm my Father worked 14 years for Mr Henery Stones. My parents were very poor / when I was a month old the new house was finish at the Wick farm. and there my parents moved and resized there 6 years. I heard my parents say after they was married my Father worked for 9s 10 a week. They had hard struggle to bring up a family of 12 children. I was the middle one out of 13. one died when an infant. they brought 6 sons a 6 daughters up to men a woman. My parents were poor hard working people. I rember my father telling us children his dear Mother died when he was a tiny little boy. his poor father was a poor farm labourer he brought up a large family of 12 children at Nevendontie near Wickford. he could not afford to give his children much education. father told us children he went to work at an early age of 6 years his employment was driveing plough a crowscareing. his wages was twopence a day. all the week for one shilling. some farmers in those days were very cruel to poor little boys, if boys did not do justice to them as they thought they would thrash them cruel. there parents were afraid to speak to their masters of their unmerciful treatment to their dear little children. if they did they would soon be paid of with their little wages of 7s or 8 a week in those days which were hard days . . . .
in 1867 My parents a the family moved from Wickford to lower Dunton Hall in essex . . . while living at Dunton with my parents first of all I went to the little villiage School for 5 years. I left school at the age of 11 years. then I started work on the land. my first job was driveing 3 Horses on the plough. up a down the land with a ploughman named Mark Arber. sometimes with another ploughman named Charles

Newland. they broke me in for work for sometime on the
hardfallowground. sometimes I was set to go Birdscareing
a other jobs on the farm. My first pay was 3 a week. on the
Sabboth day I went to church. I was called after a time in
the little Choir . . . .
in the year 1875 29th of September My parents a the family
moved from Lower Dunton Hall to Langdon Hills. There
my parents started busions on their own / they opened a
general provision stores at the great House called the Slates
on top of the Hills close to the Crownhotel. My father
started a coalmerchants busions. although for a time I kept
working on the land for Mr Samuel Westwood. there I
earned 3s 6d a week. I kept with that Gentleman over a year
till I was 15 years of age. my wages rose to 5s a week. I then
left my old Master for a new one / after that I went to work
on a farm call Northlands between Vange a Stanfordlehope.
after that the farm was sold into building land sorry to know
the farm has laid dorman for many years. I might write
while I worked on that farm. the manager of that farm had
a little farm on Canveyisland. in February 1877 the two
Horseman and two ploughdrivers of Northlands farm went
to Canveyisland for a week to till the land. I was one of the
ploughdrivers. it was the first time me leaveing home in my
life / the two men a we two boys started for the Island on
the Monday in our glee, we all left our homes well a hearty
with our horses a waggons a ploughs. we all arrived at the
Island close to Southbenfleet at night the same day / there
lodgeings was found for us all for the week. we all slept the
first night sound a well. on the next day we all rose early.
being Tuesday we all started after having our breakfast with
the horses a ploughs to plough the fields. we kept on all that
day till night come on / then we all took our horses home
and stabled them up for the night. then we all went home
to our lodgeings / we all washed ourselves a partook of tea
together that evening all in our usal health a strength / after
tea the two Horsemen named Moses Hammond a George
Franklin went to the publichouse called the Sluice on that
Island. they stopped there till nearly closeing time / we two
boys named John a Robert Hockleys although both the same
surnames we were no relations to eachother. we both sat up
that evening a little while a then went to bed to retire for the

night. we both got on our knees a said our form of prayer
as we was taught to say. then we got in bed a went to sleep.
after a long time our mates the two men come home at late
hour. they woke we boys up a started playing with us. they
appeared the worst for drink. they undressed themselfes a
got into bed like the brute beast without kneeling on their
knees to spray (sic) the light was put out a we all went to
sleep till 20 minutes to 4 oclock the next morning / all of a
sudden one of our mates woke us up with the Deathrattles
in his throat. my mate being a boy giving to laugh at most
everything that pleased him roared right out in laughfter all
feeling alarmed. the other man called out to the Dyeing man
/ Moses /three times. no answer come from his lips / then
the man Franklin called out in fright to my mate, light a
light Bob, soon as he struck the match a lighted the candle.
he drew his last breath. we was all struck with terrour. we
all jumped out of bed a called the Landlady up she ran in
our bedroom terrourstricken. a held a lookingglass over his
mouth. taking Gods name in vain said hes gone. we all
bolted out the room with fright. this death happened on the
14th day of February 1877 on Wedensday called Vallentines
day.
I was afraid to go to bed the next night. fearing death might
come a call me away. I knew I was not ready to die. it upset
us all that week. I longed for the last day of the week to
come so that I might return home to my parent. at last it
came. we all returned home on the Saturday with our horses
and plougs a wagons. the first Wagon brought the coffin his
Horses the ones he used to drive for many years. he was the
head horseman the two men were good sound straitup
ploughman / well we all three out of four arrived back to
LangdonHills again. the other one left home with us well a
hearty. but he was brought back a Corpse / as he lived so
he died / as the tree falls so must it lie. as the man lives so
must he die / as the man dies such must he be. all through
the days of eternity . . . .
1876 a peice of ground was bought in the wood on the top
of Langdon Hills near the School/there the new Church was
built. Father a me a others helped cart the materiels such as
stones a bricks a timber . . . in 1877 on July the 2nd the
Church was opened by one of the Bishops with the help of

some of the Clergymen of the Church of England. I was one in the choir with a few others. we had new black gows with white robes placed on us a special hymns a Psalms was sung for the ocasion . . . .

I was favoured to be one of the first with the old church clerk Mr Monk to help ring the 1st new Bell 1877. the 2nd Bell came in eastertime in 1879. then the clerk a me rung the Bells for annother year till 1880 then the 3rd one came along . . . then the question was raised again about the great tennor Bell . . . after the great Bell was hung a finished it was ready to be rung with the other three / the beautiful Bell was full of music. when all 4 Bells were rung the first time they sounded miles away . . . when they all are ringing properly. they shak the very tower. a echo a reecho throug the woods for miles round . . . .

now I might write and let my readers know that all my ceremonies and forms that I went through was comming to an end. I might say my parent and we children moved again from the top of the Hills to the other end of the parish called Drystreet Langdon Hills. there my parents opened again a generelprovisionstores. I stayed at home there in that part with my parents for some length of time . . . I still kept working for my father till May the next year 1882. the time came at last I was obloiged to leave home. although I am sorry to write to let my readers know that my father and me could not get on very well together as I was treated as an odd one at times while under their care. and likewise by some of my own Brothers and Sisters. I was despised by them in their own eyes. I was one of the least of my fathers family. but I have proved as it is written in the Psalms. when thy father and Mother forsake thee the Lord will take thee up . . . it was in May the 15th 1882 on the Monday morning my father said to me you had better go and find another master. I said alright father. I left home there at once. never said goodbye to Mother neither to any of them at home. so away I goes. Not knowing when I started from home where I was going to. as I was wandering about away from home not knowing what to do nor where to go. a voice whispered in my ear. go and see your Brother Samuel. I obeyed the voice. so away I went where my Brother and his Wife lived. I kept on till I found them. they were living then at Ramsden

Crays. I went to them in trouble. it was the 1st time of me leaveing home for good. my poor father and some of my own Brothers a Sisters said I never should be any good. and I never should be able to get my own living. and that I never should be able to earn more than a shilling a day. so I was jeered and sneered. and disowned by some of being called their Brother especially when they was among the gentry . . . .

Now coming back to my Brother Samuel. soon as I found their house where they lived. I knocked at the door. and I found his dear Wife at home. I was soon invited in. she was very pleased to see me. I received from her a hearty welcome. it was the first time I saw her after her conversion. she soon told me what the dear Lord had done for her and her dear husband a her dear children. she told me how the Lord had saved her soul. and her husbands soul. and her Brothers soul. all on one Sunday in July in 1881 in an old upper room on Ramsden Heath. she also told me of Gods healing power how the dear Lord had healed her and her husband and children through the laying on of hands and the anointing with oil in Jesus Name through the prayer of faith according to the scripture. I write to let my readers know that my dear Sister in laws Brother was a plough driver with me at the Duntonhalls farms his name was Harry Crick. his parents and the family came from Suffolk. well while that Afternoons conversation was going on with my Sister in law in came my Brother Samuel from his work. who was working then at Mr Jacksons. Ramsden Bellhouse. it was the first time I saw him after his conversion. I tell you all who read this when he came in the door of his house. and when he saw me his face was full of smiles. and his clean shaveing face shoned and beamed with the Glory of God in him and his eyes sparkled with delight. and his words vibrated on his tongue. he shook hands with me heartly and said how are you Brother John I am please to see you. I utterd in return Im well thank you. and how are you. he said Im well thank God. I dont remember hearing anyone exspressing it in that language before. I looked at him with both of my eyes with amezement . . . .

After my dear Brother had a little talk with me about the Lords goodness to him and his family. we all had our tea

together. and I took notice before eating and drinking they
asked Gods Blessing on the food that we was about to
receive. while having our tea together. we got in conversation about leaving home. I told them how I left home and
that my parents did not know where I was. feeling a bit
uneasy there I said I think I shall be going home now. they
persuade me to stop the night with them so that I might go
and look for work the nex morning. so I came to the decision
that I would sleep there that night. then again my Brother
and Sister talked to me about the Lord. and give me good
advice to give my heart unto the Lord. they said they believe
the Lord would provide for me a find me work.
on that evening her Brother Harry Crick came down from
his lodgings. he was lodging with two dear good Christian
people a Brother and Sister Bailey. [Brother Elijah Bailey of
Ramsden Heath] when Harry saw me one may be sure how
he felt. we had not met for many years till that night . . .
Harry soon began to tell me what the dear Lord had done
for his soul. so again they all preached to me about the love
of the Saviour. then Samuel and Harry spoke together about
finding work for me so I could keep with them. so arange-
ments was made for me to go with Harry the next morning
where he worked. and that was at Nevendon to Mr Abram
Orffins farm. well the time came when we all bid one-
theother good night. so Harry left us. I might write just
before we retired to rest for the night as I was to sleep
downstairs for a makeshift that night. before my dear
Brother Samuel and his dear Wife went upstairs to rest. they
acted very wisely. they decided to pray together for me
downstairs the first night I was there. so we all kneeled
down together on our knees. Samuel prayed first. I never
heard such a prayer in all my life. they both prayed for me
in earnest they asked the Lord to trouble me by his holy
Spirit that night. and a lot of other good things. they asked
the Lord to provide work for me the next morning and
make out ways for me so that I might keep with them. I
might say when Samuel finish. then his wife prayed. and a
earnest prayer was offered up from her heart for me in the
same manner as her husband had already prayed. I was
affraid they was going to ask me to pray. for I knew I could
not pray. I had been used to say forms of prayers which I

had learned to say by heart from my lips only. I was thankful
they did not ask me. so we all got up from our knees. and
they both bid me good night. and I bid them good night
. . . .

after we was all gone to bed and the light was put out while
I was laying on the sofa downstairs all alone in the dark and
trying to go to sleep. a strange awful feeling come over me.
I began to tremble and shake. the bedcloths seem to go up
and down. it seemed as if something was crawling over me.
I turned my face to the wall and I coved the bedcloths over
my head. My Brother Samuel and his Wifes prayers rung in
my ears for hours that night. the words they prayed kept
ringing in my ears over a over again. I was afraid to look
out of the couch that I was laying on for fear I might see the
Devil in the Room. I was afraid to call my Brother up as I
was afraid to stir. as the poet says. I was afraid to leave my
place and yet afraid to stay. again I was afraid I was going
to die that night for I felt if I had died I should have dropped
into Hell. to make the matter worse for me there was an
americian Clock hung over my head on the wall. as it struck
the hours in solom tone it seemed as if I heard my own
Death Bell tolling. I heard it strike 10 the first hour. I laid
another hour trembling a shakeing and still their prayers kept
ringing in my ears. I dreaded the Clock to strike. then again
it struck 2 awful tones . . . presenty to my horror right in
the middle of the night that Clock struck 12 awful solom
tones. I could not felt worse than I did if I had heard my
own Death Bell tolling. I felt like a crimnel as if sentence of
death had been passed upon me. again I laid awake 3 more
hours in that terrible plight. so I laid awake 6 hours. I heard
the Clock strike 10.11.12.that night and 1.2.3. the next
morning. then daylight began to come. it was then the 16th
of May. then I went into a sound sleep till 5 oclock that
morning . . . then I rose up from the couch where I had laid
down for the night. and dressed myself. after I partook of
a peice of food and drank a cup of tea. I then left Brother
Samuel to go with Harry Crick to his work at Nevendon to
Mr Abram Offins farm . . . .

well we at last reach the farm we both went to the Gentle-
mans house. he came out. Harry said goodmorning Sir. he
ask him if he could find me as I was his friend a job for me.

I was born in the year 1861 on the 7 day of September in the village of Wickford in Essex, at that time a bungalow was being built for my parents at Wickford Wick. at that farm my Father worked 14 years for Mr Henry Stone. My parents were very poor when I was a month old the new house was finish at the Wick farm. and there my parents moved and stayed there 6 years. I heard my parents say after they was married my Father worked for 9.10 a week they had hard struggle to bring up a family of 12 children. I was the middle one out of 13 one died when an infant. they brought 6 sons a 6 Daughters up to men a woman, my parents were poor hard working people, I rember my fathers telling us children his dear Mother died when he was a tiny little boy. his poor father was a poor farm labourer he brought up a large family of 12 children at Nevendon tie near Wickford, he could not afford to give his children much education. father told us children he went to work at an early age of 6 years his employment was driveing plough a crow-scareing. his wages was twopence a day. all the week for one shilling. some farmers in those days were very cruel to poor little boys, if boys did not do justice to them as they thought they would thrash them cruel. there parents were afraid to speak to their masters of their unmerciful treatment to their dear little children. if they did they would soon be paid of with their little wages of 7 a 8 a week in those days which were hard days. as time went on my parent was married, they got a poor comfatable little home together, as years went on they strugled a worked hard together a brought up a large family of 12 children. I might say a few years after my parents were married, my poor Grandfather died at a little bungalow at Nevendontie. he was an independent member of a little Chappel then in the Runwell road Wickford. there his remains was buried in the little graveyard where that little chapel was then where he worshiped many years. I was named after my dear old Grandfather at his whish.

Right: *The picture shows Brother Isaac Anderson with his wife.* Above: *He is shown at his work in Southend (see p.115)*

but I was in hopes he would say no. because I dreaded going
back to Brother Samuels house to sleep the next night . . .
yet on the other hand I did not want to go back to my
parents. so the Gentleman considered it over in his mind for
a while. presently he said Yes I could go and work with him
meaning Harry. I felt bad. yet after sometime I felt glad.
so away we went to the field spudding the weeds out from
the barley that was sown with young clover. Harry was full
of smiles and please because I had a job with him. that was
moor than I was. we worked all that day. I had a job to keep
up with Harry as he was one on side of the stech [ridge of
ploughland between two drainage furrows] and me the oth-
erside. he kept preaching and singing to me all the day. but
when I got a little behind he so kindly put his spud on my
side and helped me up. I remember one piece of a hymn he
sung it was. my happy soul is free. the Lord has pardend
me. Hallelujah to God and the Lamb/he said you cant say so
can you John but I made no answer. I might say there was
two parties working in that field. one little party was Gods
children I mean by adoption. the other party was of the
Devil. I noticed when mealtimes came round. the good party
sat together and ask Gods blessing on their food. while the
other wicked party which was the biggest. was cursing eachother and the people of God. well I knew they was not right
so I sat with the good party. the time came round to go
home. when I reached home to my Brother and Sister they
want to know how I had been getting on. when they heard
I had got a job they felt so please and thankful to God. if
ever prayer was heard and answered for any one. they was
for me . . . .
I was affraid to go to bed the next night . . . what to do I
did not know. well I went again to lay me down on the
couch. but thank God he was merciful and kind to me that
night. and I slept beautiful a sound till the morning. till it
was times for me to arise/again I went on Wedensday morning to work with Harry my mate. he preached a sung hymns
to me at times dureing that day. he invited me to go to
Chapel with him that evening as they held meetings every
Wedensday evenings. at last that days work come to a close.
so we again reached home in safety. after tea was over Harry
called for me to go with him to Chapel. so at last he prevailed

upon me to go a so did Samuel. so away we all went to the
Peculiarpeoples Chapels on Ramsdenheath which was over
two miles. it was 2 miles from our work to our home a over
2 miles to the Chapel. make in all over 4 miles to go from
our work. at last we reach the Chapel. we all went in. I took
a seat behind. when we all went in they was sining a beautiful
hymn . . . I never heard such singing before. over and over
again they sang that beautiful chorous

      My beautiful home, My beautiful home.
      in the land where the Glorrified ever shall roam
      where Angels Bright wear crowns of light.
      My home is there my home is there.

as the meeting went on the elder [Elder Joseph Elsdon of
Ramsden Heath] rose to speak. he was a homely looking
plain man/ he was a poor hard working man who laboured
on the land. he used to wear a green smock. as some used
to say. an overall which covered all. he preached the old old
story of Jesus and his love. he told his own experience in his
plain simple way. and the Brothers and Sisters. one by one
spoke their experience and told out the greatgoodness of the
Lord to them. how he had saved their souls a healed their
bodies. and so it went on till it was time to sing the closeing
hymn. that was the end of that meeting. well after the service
was over they shook hands with me one by one and said
they was pleased to see me and asked me to come again. one
young man who knew me when living with his parents on
Langdon Hills was delighted to see me. he had just giving
his heart to the Lord previously. he said to me I am pleased
to see you John come again and give your heart to the Lord
that will be the best days work you ever done in your life.
so we bid each other good night. I left them all and went
straitaway to the whitehorse publichouse and drank a glass
of beer/when I came out I met harry a his own Sister a
others. I said to them I was dry but they said I was trying
to wash it down . . . .

Harry kept on preaching to me in the daytime. Brother
Samuel a his Wife kept preaching to me at night. although
at times I tryed to withstand them. and said they was not
written in the Bible the important things they told me.
specially the healing power but they soon opened the Bible
before my eyes and showed me where to find the passages

. . . so I had to give it up at last as I felt for a bad job. at last Saturday night come round. I received my first 5 days wages 2s 2d a day. one may be sure how pleased I felt when I received that nice sum of money for the first time in my experience. then after haveing tea I started to go home to my parents to Langdon hills . . .

they all received me kindly and wanted to know how I had been getting on and where I had been working. I told them all about it a that I had been working at Mr Abram Offins farm Nevendon. so some of my Brothers said in a carcastic manner. how much money have you been getting Jack. I said boldly 2s 2d a day and Im going to have 13 Bob a week/ what they said/all that. another Brother said who was in my favour. he said to his other Brothers in a cunning way I thought you said Jack wouldnt get moor than a shilling a day and he spoke up for me while others jeered me. but dear Mother was pleased to see me . . . we all had a nice conversation together that Sunday evening. then after supper we all retired to rest for the night.

when Sunday morning come round we all rose to have our breakfast then after that I put on my best cloths to go to my Church again. when I reach the Church. there I met all my mates the Choir Boys away we all goes up into the tower we all had a nice talk together we was all very fond of each other. of course they wanted to know how I had been getting on dureing that week I had been away from home. I told them all about it. amd that I was going to leave them all for good . . . they said to me I should never think you are going to be a Chapelman are you I said I am. I start preaching to them before I got converted myself/ after a little moor talk together/ we all started again to ring our Bells for the afternoon service / but I could not get on with them as I had done before at othertimes/the beautiful Bells did not seem to have the same charms for me as they did in former times/ I can truthfully say that I set my heart an affections upon those Beautiful Church Bells. I adored them a nearly worshipped them but all that was gone from me at last . . . I might say it was my last time I rung those Bells. so we the Choir Boys went again in the vestry to put on our gowns. that was the last time with me. I never wore them any more after that/ again for the last time I took my seat in the choir

with the rest of the Boys/ that was in the last Sunday of May
1882 . . . then l left Langdon Hills that Sunday evening and
then made my way back to Ramsden Crays to my dear
Brothers a Sisters home . . . after having our supper we all
retired to rest for the night. when the morning came round
I arose from my bed. then drank a cup of tea then of I went
to work with Harry . . . .

It was in the year 1882 in May the 31st on that Wedensday
night about 9 oclock in the Peculiar peoples Chapel on Ramsden Heath when God for Christ sake pardend all my sins
. . . many prayers was being offered up to the dear Lord
every morning and evening for me that I might be saved.
and I thank God those prayers was heard and answerd at
last. but O how Satat did try to stop me from giving my
heart to God. he suggested many things to my mind. he
showed me the Church Bells and the black a white gowns
and the pressents. that I should have to forfiet. one certain
thing he pictured up before me was a half a crown/ at the
anniversary of the opening of Langdonhills Church. all we
Choir Boys was to receive one halfacrown apiece. that would
be on July the 2nd it was just over a month that I had got
to wait. before my halfcrown was due to me. well I said to
Brother Samuel you might let me have my half a crown first
/meaning when I had received my halfcrown in a months
time first. then I would give my heart to the Lord. and join
those happy people/ Samuel looked at me strait in the face.
said to me in a solom voice. having his eyes still fixed on
me. John. what. lose your Soul for half a crown. oh those
words he said to me went in like a dagger to my heart . . .
what words to find to answer him. I did not know . . . then
dear reader you see satan tryed to rob of giving my heart to
God. for the sake of a half a crown. but Satan did not show
me what I should gain if I would give up my half crown
and other things that was promised me. but prais God I
came to the decision at last that I would give up my halfacrown for a whole Crown/and that was a Crown of Bright
Glory that fadeth not away.

Well comeing back to Wedensday May 31. Harry spoke
kindly to me that day while we was at work together in the
field. he tryed to induce me to give my heart to Jesus that
night. he invited me again to come to Chapel with him that

Wednesday evening. I promised him I would. I believe I said
to him that day. you might get up and tell the people I want
to be saved tonight Harry will you. he said all right John.
not thining he was going to do it . . . well leaveing that for
a while. as Harry and I had finish work for the day. we and
all the other men came home together/ as we all was walking
in the road home together we got talking about going to
Chapel that night at Ramsden Heath/ while the Peculiars
was inviteing me to go with them to Chapel that night.
satan was working through some of his agents to perwswade
me not to go with them people. first I said I would not go.
then the dear people of God said to me. you come with us
John. then I come again to the decision . . . I made up my
mind that I would go and give my heart to the Lord that
night. satans party said I can hear they will have him to
night. then we all parted in a three want way [a parting of
three ways] and bid each other good night. so we all made
haste home to wash and have our teas. as we had already
walked 2 miles from our work. and we had got to walk over
2 miles after having our teas before we got to the Chapel.
so we put ourselves about sharp a had our teas. then after
tea they called for me to go to Chapel with them so we all
went together . . . .
well at last we reach the Chapel at Ramsden Heath. I followed Harry Crick and Elijah Bailey right up the other end
of the Chapel close to the Desk there I kneeled down on my
knees with Harry. there I made a short prayer to myself. all
the words I could utter was. Lord save me to night over a
over again did I utter those words from my heart. then after
we got up of our knees. I glanced at the preacher his name
was Joseph Elsdon. presently the Servant of God rose from
his seat. . . he said let us sing together the 583rd Hymn
. . . over the top of that Hymn (in the hymnbook) is

Hell

and the words out of Bible are these you will find them in
the 23. Chapter of St Matthew Gospel 33 verse
               escape the damnation of hell . . . .
he give out that hymn verse by verse very solom. oh how
bad I felt had I died then while they was singing that won-

derful solom hymn I should have dropped into hell where
hope nor mercy could have reached me. but thanks be to
God he had mercy on me that night. they sung the last verse
over a over again. once again I charge you stop for unless
you warning take. ere you are aware youl drop into the
burning lake.

after the hymn was sung they all took their seats. again the
Elder rose from his seat and told out his own experience
what the Lord had done for him soul and body. the Gospel
was faithfully preach that night. after the Elder sat down
then others rose up and told out the goodness of the Lord
. . . especially Harry he told out the greatgoodness of the
Lord to him. how he saved his soul a healed his body. I took
special notice what he said. knowing that he and me was
ploughdrivers together. and that both of our fathers work
on the same farms together at Upper a Lower Dunton Halls.
he kept on speaking till at last he brought me in. he told out
how I had come on purpose to give my heart to the Lord he
spoke with an earnest desire that I might be saved that night.
when the time was up the minister rose up to give out the
closeing hymn. the beautiful hymn was number 848. The
words over the hymn was

Heaven

part of the verse of the Scripture was 15th Chapter of luke
7th verse. joy shall be in heaven over one sinner that repen-
teth more than over ninety and nine just persons which need
no repentance. the hymn was. what tongue can tell. what
heart conceive. the bliss that reigns above. when first the
sinner feels his need. of Jesus pardening love. while the dear
saints of God was sining that beautiful hymn from their
hearts. verse by verse over a over again rejoiceing in the
God of their salvation. I felt bad. the more the dear people
of God rejoiced. the worse I felt. for I felt like one that was
on the prescipeice of hell. yet I was on the verge of Salvation.
the dear Servant of God had his eyes on me. he seeing how
I was hanging my head down and how bad I felt. he put his
hand so kindly to me over the desk where he was standing.
he said to me how are you mate. right before all the little
congregation. I raised my head a little. and mumbled out

something feeling worse than ever. one may be sure how all
the peoples eyes were set on me the preacher still holding
my hand. while the dear people was still sining and praiseing
God down that beautiful hymn. when they came to that
beautiful verse. the gates wide open to receive the newborn
child of heaven. the saints below their voices raised/Glory
to God is given. the man of God said to me. praise the Lord
mate. I said faintly in return. praise the Lord. one said say
blessed Jesus thou art my Saviour. I said a little louder.
blessed Jesus thou art my Saviour. still they kept sining on.
and still they kept asking me to confess Jesus to be my
Saviour from my heart. then I shouted out these word from
the bottom of my heart. I do Believe in my Lord and my
God. his name is worthy to be praised. there and then the
burden of my heart rolled away.I sang I praised the Lord
with all my new Brothers a Sisters. truly as they sung in that
verse. the saints below their voices raised/Glory to God was
given. praise God the Angels in heaven was rejoiceing. and
the saints on earth was rejoiceing over me. I could sing then
with Harry. My happy soul is free the Lord hath pardend
me Hallelujah to God a the Lamb. I went to Ramsden Heath
that night a wretched sinner. for I felt like the Apostel Paul
had written. O wretched man that I am who shall deliver
me from the body of this death/ I thank God through Jesus
Christ our Lord. so I went to chapel a lost all my sins a I
came back a happy young lad . . . .
after I reached home with my brother and Sister we got
talking about the goodness of the Lord till we all went to
bed. then I laid me down that night safe in the arms of Jesus
. . . I laid me down and slept that night feeling all was well
soul and body. when the morning came I rose early from
my bed and dressed myself. and down on my knees I bowd
before my heavenly Father. and prayed to him in Jesus name.
to thank him for his protecting care and sweet sleep through
the past night. then I prayed for his preserveing care through
the day that layed before me and that he would give me
grace to live to him that day without sin. then I rose up. and
after having a cup of tea and a little food. I started of again
with brother Harry Crick to go to work. I felt then I was
his new brother in Christ Jesus. I felt like a new lad in a new
world. old things had passed away and all things had become

new. I was a new creature in Christ Jesus. we both went along the road that morning happy in the Lord. I felt like the Psalmist. he brought me up out of a horrible pit and out of the mirey clay. set my feet on a rock. establish my goeings. and put a new song in my mouth. even praises unto the Lord . . . .

III William Heddle

Born Redland, Stromness, Orkney 1846.
Came to Maldon, Essex 1864.
Joined the Peculiar People at Southend 1873.
Ordained an Elder at Southend 1877.
Supreme Bishop of the Peculiar People 1901.
Retired 1942.
Died 1948, at Southend, aged 101 years 11 months.

The following extracts are taken from *A brief account of my Life and Experience* by William Heddle (privately printed at Southend, 1930).

My father was a tailor, and had nineteen employees, but he lost his health and took to farming, and hired "Redland" (Stromness). I was the first of the family of eight that was born at "Redland"; there were three older than me. We were poor, although our grandfathers were both well-to-do. My father was so weakly that he always had to have a foreman.

When a child I was very ill, and had yellow jaundice very badly; although there were fears that I would die, God spared me. I had only a poor education, as my brother John, who was older than me, had a weak or withered arm, and was sent to Stromness to a boarding school.

When I was quite a little lad I had to go out in the dark

winter mornings to thrash with the flail. We had to light our lamp with flint and steel; open lamp with fish oil and wick.

When I was fourteen years old I acted as head man at "Redland", and it was God's mercy I did not lose my life while trying to break in a tall young horse.

I also worked at "Rosehill", quarrying stones, carting stones, and helping to build "Rosehill".

When I was sixteen years old I worked as a stone mason during the summer, building the Water Mill, Carston; also a gentleman's house the north end of Stromness . . .

When I was seventeen years and eight months old I left home for England. I signed the teetotal pledge at my dear parents' request, as a safeguard, before leaving home. I left home on the 19th April 1864 . . .

I came to Maldon, Essex. My master (Mr Binning) was far from being a good man. He got a lot of work out of me. John Hennan, one of his travellers who showed me up a great part of my rounds, told me except I gave up being a teetotaller I would not get on at the trade. However, I said to myself I would give up the trade rather than my teetotalism, so I kept to my pledge. My master promised me if I increased my takings to a certain sum per week, he would make me a present of a good watch. This I attempted and did, and after waiting some while for my watch, I mentioned the fact to my master. He said if I kept on he would not only give me a watch, but give me an albert also, as he had not forgotten his promise. However, I got neither watch nor albert, nor a certain commission on the sale of a number of jackets . . .

Mr James Hamilton, of Chelmsford, was deeply interested in me, when I was at Maldon, and knowing how I was treated by my master, offered me a situation, so I gave my master, Mr Binning, three months' notice that I was going to leave him. I was with him 3½ years.

I went to Chelmsford and entered into an agreement with Mr Hamilton to serve him twelve months without any salary, if he would guarantee me into business – which he did. I travelled rounds, part of which he bought of Thomas Currie, and David Halliday, and John Craig, and some of his own.

Mr Hamilton was a man of honour and dignity, Church

Deacon, and Superintendent of the Sunday School of the Congregational Chapel, Baddow Road, Chelmsford. He persuaded me to become a Sunday School teacher, and afterwards he persuaded me to become a Church member as an example to the lads. This I also did. I had no difficulty in becoming a member, as I was not asked if I was saved, or converted, or born again. I simply set forth the belief I had about Jesus Christ having died for sinners, and my desire to live a good life . . . .

Mr Hamilton put me into business in October 1868. I married in September 1870, and came to live in Southend, and my wife and I worshipped at the Cliff Town Congregational Church, and paid our pew rent there. Mr Wannicott, the minister there, very much wanted me to have my Church membership transferred to Southend, but as I had become quite dissatisfied about my state and salvation, I declined to apply for it, and told him I wanted to join Christ first. I wanted to experience what it was to be born again.

After a time we had a fresh minister, a Mr Williams. He soon took special notice of us, and he tried his best to get me to have my Church membership transferred, but I declined on the same grounds . . . (One) Thursday night, Mr Williams took for his lesson 2 Cor. 5ch.14v., to the end. After the service we both went into the vestry. He said: "Take a seat, and tell me how you are getting on". Neither of us sat down. I put my fingers on to the table and said: "You know your lesson to-night?" He said: "Yes; 'Therefore if any man be in Christ, he is a new creature'". I said: "Well, that's just what I want to be; so you know how I am". He did not attempt to show me how that Jesus Christ had become my substitute, and died for me; and as He had died for me that God was just and yet the justifier of whosoever believeth on Him, and accepted Him as their personal Saviour, and if I praised Him for dying for me, that the Lord would save me. Instead of that, he tried to show me that it was temptation I had got into, and he believed that if I lived right, and did my best, I would find it all right in the end. But I told him what I read in 1st John 5ch., 10v. "He that believeth on the Son of God hath the witness in himself", and that I wanted that witness. He told me I was the plainest Scotsman that ever he had met; so we had to part . . .

The Peculiar People were to hold a public meeting in the British School, High Street, Southend. I made up my mind I would, if possible, attend it in the evening. I started early on my rounds for that purpose, but hindrances one·after another came in my way. I drove my mare in the Weir pond at Fobbing, and after raising her foot and splashing the water two or three times, she lay right down in the pond. Well, I got to the meeting rather late, and they were singing a hymn with the chorus:-

> I do believe it;
> I am saved through the Blood of the Lamb.
> My happy soul is free,
> For the Lord has pardoned me,
> Hallelujah to God and the Lamb.

Oh! I felt as if I would give all I possessed if I could sing that from the bottom of my heart, as those on the platform were singing it. I did not get saved.

A Sister Anderson who was greatly interested about my salvation, after many conversations, told me quite plainly that I required to be born again, and have a knowledge of my sins forgiven. I inwardly admitted the truth of this, but I shunned her for a time; I did not think that I required such a conversion as a drunkard or a thief, although I wanted to be saved and know my sins forgiven. Brother Joseph Went [of Herongate], took considerable interest in my salvation, and after many conversations he put, I think it was a sovereign in my hand, and asked me if I *hoped* I had got it. I sighed, and said: "Well, I would say I *had* got it". He said: "Just so; he that believeth on the Son of God hath the witness in himself . . ." Aged Brother Thorogood told me I was begotten by the Word, but I required to be born of the Spirit.

On the 10th March 1873, between 6 and 7 o'clock in the evening, being all alone on the open road in the country, driving from Horndon-on-the-Hill to Bulphan Fen, wishing, longing, and praying to be saved – realising I was lost; I was a sinner, needing saving as much as the poor drunkard; . . . and trying to bring passages of Scripture to my mind for the purpose of seeing whether I could gain or lay hold on the Salvation of God. I cannot say how many passages came to my mind, but I well remember John 3ch., 16v., came and passed without my gaining salvation, and after this the words, as if they came from Heaven: *That he tasted death for every man*. Up went my right hand and arm as I shouted: "Praise the Lord then; He died for me". There and then God baptised me with the Holy Ghost. I praised the Lord, I blessed the Lord, I felt my sins were all forgiven, I was filled with love, joy and peace . . .

(So) I joined the Peculiar People, and I praise the Lord to-day for His guidance, His love, His mercy, and His grace in sparing me life, and healing me and rescuing me from death and the grave, and lengthening out my day; also healing my dear wife and rescuing her from death and the grave.

Since the Lord saved me over fifty-seven years ago, I have had many afflications, some of them of a very serious nature, very nigh unto death, but in answer to prayer, God has healed me, and restored me; praise Him! . . .

Now reverting to my young time. During the three and a half years I served Mr. Binning at Maldon, I never had a holiday, not even a half of a day.

I had one very tiring round which could not be done in less than twelve hours, walking from Maldon, carrying my orders and goods to Purleigh, Stow Maries, Cold Norton, and returning to Maldon. I started on that round many a morning before the governor was down, at times leaving home at 7 a.m., having a long walk before commencing my business, so I could get back before too late at night.

I had no holiday given me during the twelve months I served Mr. Hamilton . . . I used to rise about four o'clock on Monday morning when at Chelmsford, to get my orders ready.

On Monday morning I used to take the Parlimentary train from Chelmsford to Ingatestone, walk up and do business in the village, then walk to Stock and have dinner. I felt sometimes as if I could have done with two dinners that day. After doing business there I proceeded to Billericay. The following Monday took the "Parly" train to Brentwood and walked through Great Warley, Little Warley, Childer-ditch and East Horndon, and the next day to Stanford-le-Hope etc.

I stopped at the Hope Hotel, Southend, one night every fortnight. In those days there were no trains or carriers from

Rochford to Chelmsford on a Saturday, so it was our custom to look out for a miller's van or a brewer's van to give us a lift from Rochford to Chelmsford.

I stopped every Friday night at the Golden Lion, North Street, Rochford, three years all but a month. I had a nice little back room there, where I did my letter writing and my ledger work after I got into business . . . I was very nicely accommodated and quiet there.

One Saturday I did the town of Rochford and returned home by van or walked to Maldon, crossing Fambridge Ferry to take train to Chelmsford. The other Saturday from Rochford in the morning to Great Stambridge and Canewdon. On one occasion I hoped to happen with a miller's van, so I started to walk on the road to Chelmsford. I was not picked up at all, and had to walk all the way to Chelmsford from Rochford and Canewdon – that was an exception . . .

When I was married I came to Southend-on-Sea to live, and started business in Park Street. On Saturday nights we kept open till eleven o' clock (at that time of day shopkeepers kept open late). I tried to get this altered, but could not – earlier closing was opposed on the plea that people came out of the public houses at eleven p.m. and made several purchases. Then, failing to get others to close, I did not want to show myself in opposition by closing my shop.

Before I bought a horse it was a rule for me to have a tremendous day on Mondays; for the miles I have walked carrying my orders and goods . . . After I bought my horse I used to feed it extra on Sundays for the work it had to do on the Mondays and Tuesdays. I got my goods and orders ready on the Saturday and loaded up that night ready for starting on Monday morning [i.e he loaded up on Saturday so as not to do work on a Sunday].

One week on Monday morning, I started and went through Pitsea, Vange, Fobbing, Corringham, Stanford-le-Hope, Horndon-on-the-Hill, on to Bulphan Fen, staying that night at Bulphan.

In the summertime at Bulphan I used to get up and go to the west side of the Fen before breakfast – because I had certain customers there that went out to field work pea-picking and gleaning – then got back and had breakfast, put my horse to and go round the other part of the Fen, and

then start off for Great Warley and Little Warley, Childer-
ditch, East Horndon, and back to the corner of Bulphan
Parish, then over Langdon Hills home to Southend. Very
often I had a job to keep awake these journeys I did alone.

Another week on Monday morning, in the winter time,
I have been at the top of the hill, Eastwood Road, Rayleigh
(where the wind-mills used to stand) when the sun was
rising, because I had to go so far before I commenced business (nearly seven miles before sunrise). That night I stopped
at the White Hart, Billericay; on Tuesday do business in
Billericay, then round about to Ramsden Heath and Down-
ham etc. etc. When I had a couple of large cases of boots
come in, after the shop was closed and the counters cleared,
I used to have a coffee supper, then unpack the boots, examine them, sort them by sizes, and mark them off till 1.30 or
perhaps 2 o'clock a.m; dear mother helping as well, the
children being asleep . . .

Once I was young, now I am old, and see that experience
teaches knowledge, but I give God all the praise, for God
moves in a mysterious way, His wonders and love to show.
So I rejoice I have been favoured to successfully put my six
sons into business, four sons-in-law and one nephew.

Now what shall I say? what can I say? . . . But . . .
exclaim glory, honour, praise and power be unto our Lord
for ever, for all his mercy, love and grace to us, soul and
body; preserving our lives, saving our souls, and healing us
and our dear ones (in answer to prayers) of so many diseases
and afflictions; blessing us with health and strength, preserving our senses and reason, faculties and powers; and blessing
us with a glorious hope of Immortality, through Jesus Christ
our Lord. Hallelujah!

A Selection of hymns from the Peculiar People's Hymn Book

Dear brethren, come, let's talk awhile
  About ourselves and grace;
'Tis good at times to weigh ourselves,
  And look into the glass.

We all do have our trials still,
  And need God's help, 'tis true;
But have we stood and done God's will,
  And so got safely through?

A priv'lege God's bestowed on us,
  Who know we're born again;
That, as our day our strength shall be,
  This promise shall remain.

This promise to God's sons is giv'n,
  And others have no claim;
Then may we prove we're heirs of heav'n
  By trusting in His name.

Suppose your trials have been great,
  And now swell more and more,
Our Father's nigh, His promise sweet,
  You may expect a show'r.

But if the furnace should be hot,
  And deep in waters cast,
We have the hope, God by His grace,
  Will bring us home at last.

(Attributed to John Benton.)

Strait is the gate through which we pass,
  And narrow is the way;
That leads to everlasting bliss,
  And realms of endless day.

The unclean cannot walk therein,
  Because the way is pure;
We must be free from every sin,
  Or else God's wrath endure.

Repent, believe, the Scriptures say,
  With water be baptized;
The Saviour bore your sins away,
  When He was crucified.

This is the entrance of the way,
  That leads from earth to heaven,
If you the Gospel will obey,
  Your sins shall be forgiven.

Christ, who was infinitely wise,
  The gospel plan ordained;
It was, believe and be baptised,
  Or else you must be damned.

This is the only way to heaven,
  All others lead to hell;
This gospel was by Jesus given,
  And is unalterable.

God's curse will rest upon the man
  Who does false doctrine teach;
Or goes contrary to this plan,
  Or other gospel preach.

And now this gospel's preached to you,
  You are without excuse;
All, it commands you sure must do,
  Or else endure the curse.

                                    (*Author unknown*)

Come brethren dear, let's join and sing
The praises of our heavenly king,
Who sets our spirits on a flame,
That we should glorify his name.
   O what a happy people,
   Who is so blest as we?

Our sins are pardoned, we are free,
Jesus, we now belong to thee;
We've got the witness now within,
And know that we are born again.
   O what . . .

We raise our voice to Thee and sing,
Glory and honour to our King;
Our Father smiles to hear our song,
When it is in the spirit sung.
   O what . . .

Since we have last assembled here,
What has each member had to bear!
Both trials and temptations too;
But Jesus brings us safely through.
   O what . . .

                                        (*Author unknown*)

An Affectionate Hint Respecting Public Worship
(for private meditation).

The great Jehovah, from His glorious throne,
Stoops down to make his love and mercy known;
And bids the chosen tribe of Israel meet
Where he reveals the glories of His feet.

He sends his heralds forth in Jesus' name,
To publish peace and pardoning love proclaim;
Yes, he goes with them, and applies His word,
And makes it life and health and joy afford.

Where, then, is that ungrateful sinner found,
Who slights and disregards the Gospel sound?
Who, when Jehovah in His courts draws near
Neglects within those holy courts to appear?

Can those who once have tasted Jesus' grace
Choose to be absent when he shows His face?
Shall a few drops of rain or dirty road
Prevent their public intercourse with God?

Shall gossip calls or some inferior things
Detain, when summoned by the King of kings?
Blush, brethren, at the God-insulting thought!
And prove in conduct you are better taught.

Remember, every time the house of prayer
Is open for the saints, the Lord is there!
To hold communion with the heaven-born race,
And give them from his fullness grace for grace.

Let not such sacred seasons be forgot –
Say to each worldly care, "Detain me not!"
A feast is held, and I must share a part;
I'll not be robbed, nor grieve my pastor's heart.

See! Satan's slaves to scenes of riot go,
By day or night, through rain or hail or snow!
And shall some visitor or worldly care
Detain believers from the house of prayer?

Forbid it, Lord, revive Thy people's zeal;
The lukewarm plague among Thy children heal;
Ye heirs of bliss, whom Jesus often meets,
Whene'er His house is open, fill your seats.

Jehovah loves the temples of His grace
More than the tents of all His chosen race:
Blest is the man whose seeking spirit waits
On all the means of grace in Zion's gates.

Bear with me, while I say the crime is great
Of those who practise coming very late;
As if God's service was by far too long,
And they omit the first and closing song.

Shall chapel doors rattle and umbrellas move*
To show how you the service disapprove?
Disturbing those who come to praise the Lord?
And even while they listen to His Word?

A little less indulgence in the bed –
A little more contrivance in the head –
A little more devotion of the mind –
Would quite prevent your being so behind!

Suppose an earthly prince should condescend
To bid you to his banquet as a friend,
Would you not try all means within your power
To be in court at the appointed hour?

Shall such attention to a worm be given,
And be refused to the God of Heaven?
Who can expect to be by Jesus blest,
If absent when He comes to greet His guests?

O what a pleasing sight it would afford
If when the elder says, "Let's praise the Lord",†
Each seat was occupied, and all the throng
Were waiting to unite in their first song.

My brethren this might mostly be the case,
If we were lively in the Christian race;
Then every hindrance would be laid aside,
To see and hear of Jesus crucified.

---

* In the original 1860 edition, this line read: "Shall pew doors rattle, hats and pattens move".
† This line originally read: "If when the clerk says, 'Let us praise the Lord.' "

If you complain you have so far to come
Set out a little sooner from your home;
But those who dwell hard-by have no excuse,
Except in idleness, or sleep or use.

I grant, lest I should seem to be severe,
There are domestic cases here and there,
Age – illness – service – things quite unforeseen,
To censure which I surely do not mean.

But such will not (unless I greatly err)
Among the prudent very oft occur;
And when they do, you surely should endeavour,
To come at last – 'tis better late than never!

(Attributed to J. Irons.)

Peculiar are the Saints,
  And God does them esteem,
Though numerous are their wants,
  They all things have in Him.
He is their treasure and their joy;
Nor shall they ever starve or die.

Loved from eternity,
  And chosen in the Lamb,
The eternal one in three –
  Jehovah, great I am.
Himself hath bound, by holy ties,
To take them up beyond the skies.

Peculiar is the grace,
  Which makes their bliss secure;
Its beauties none can trace,
  Nor know its saving power.
None but this little favoured few
Can know what endless love can do.

Bought with the Blood of Christ –
   Peculiar price indeed –
Their Lord becomes their Priest,
   And they from sin are freed.
Peculiar must the blessing be
Which makes insolvent wretches free.

Their birth is from above –
   Peculiar birth indeed;
Begotten not of blood,
   But of immortal seed.
From Christ, their head, their life proceeds,
And to Him it most surely leads.

They live and live to God,
   A life that's known by few;
Their Father's staff and rod,
   Support and comfort too.
Abide in Christ, they cannot die,
For hell can ne'er their life destroy.

                     (Attributed to J. Irons.)

This is the field – the world below,
In which the sower came to sow;
Jesus the wheat – Satan the tares,
For so the Word of God declares.
     And soon the reaping time will come,
     And angels shout the harvest home.

Most awful truth! and is it so –
Must all the world the harvest know?
Is every man a wheat or tare?
Then for the harvest, O prepare.
     And soon . . .

To love my sins – a saint t'appear,
To grow with wheat and be a tare,
May serve some while on earth below,
Where tares and wheat together grow.
     And soon . . .

But all who truly righteous are,
Their Father's kingdom then shall see,
Shine like the sun for ever there –
He that hath ears then let him hear.
    And soon . . .

(Author unknown)

All glory be to God on high,
Who does my daily wants supply;
Whate'er I need, his hand bestows,
He gives me food, he gives me clothes.

He gives me health and strength by day,
By night his angels near me stay;
I live and move through him I serve,
Through him alone my being have.

I'm hedged about on every side,
With mercies new I'm satisfied;
From morn till noon, from noon till eve,
And all night long I good receive.

I'm heir to yonder blest estate,
There is my God my portion great,
There waits for me a crown of gold,
And riches that can ne'er be told.

I'm but a stranger here below,
A pilgrim through this vale of woe;
But I've a house not made with hands,
In yonder realm of bliss it stands.

Thither my journey I pursue,
With strength renewed I onward go;
Until I reach my heavenly home,
Where naught but righteousness can come.

(Author unknown)

Though in the outward Church below
The wheat and tares together grow,
Jesus ere long will weed the crop,
And pluck the tares in anger up.

Will it relieve their horrors there,
To recollect their stations here?
How much they heard, how much they knew,
How long amongst the wheat they grew?

O this will aggravate their case;
They perish under means of grace;
To them the Word of life and faith
Became an instrument of death.

We seem alike when thus we meet,
Strangers might think we all are wheat,
But to the Lord's all-searching eyes
Each heart appears without disguise.

The tares are spared for various ends,
Some for the sake of praying friends,
Others the Lord, against their will,
Employs his counsels to fulfil.

But though they grow so tall and strong,
His plan will not require them long;
In harvest, when He saves His own,
The tares shall into hell be thrown.

(Author unknown)

And now, my sick, afflicted friend,
May you find comfort to the end;
Be not cast down nor pine away,
But look to Jesus by the way.

Jesus, the great Physician, can
Restore and heal both child and man,
However sad is thy complaint,
His healing power knows no restraint.

When Jesus did on earth remain,
None ever sought his help in vain;
He heal'd and cured all that came;
His healing power is still the same.

Jesus alone can comfort you,
And make your sickness slight, 'tis true;
Though he afflicts, 'tis out of love,
To make you humble like a dove.

May Jesus soothe you with his love,
And send you comfort from above,
And give you strength, and life, and health,
And fill your soul with heavenly wealth.

May Jesus watch around thy bed,
And with his arms support thy head,
Or with his word bid thee arise,
For in his word the power lies.

(Author unknown)

Chapels and meeting places of The Peculiar People

(The dates given are the dates of opening of the present chapels in each location)

Baddow, Great Closed.
Barking (Thamesview Evangelical Church, Stanley Avenue) 1961
Barling (Gospel Mission, Little Wakering Road) 1926.
Canning Town (Cliff Street Evangelical Church, Barking Road) 1959.
Chadwell Heath Closed.
Chelmsford (Grove Road Evangelical Church) 1931.
Chipping Hill Moved into Witham 1874.
Corringham (Fobbing Road) 1914.
Cressing (The Street) 1909.
Daws Heath (Western Road) 1976.
Eastwood (Leighfields Road) 1927.
Fobbing Transferred to Corringham 1914.
Foulness Island Closed.
New Brompton (Gillingham, Kent) Closed.
Gravesend Closed.
Grays (Salisbury Road) 1892.
Herongate Closed.
Hockley (Greensward Lane) 1922.
Leigh (Elm Road) 1923.
London (Bethwin Road Evangelical Church, Camberwell) 1972.
Plumstead (Woolwich) Closed.
Poplar Closed.
Prittlewell (Wallis Avenue, Colchester Road) 1904.
Ramsden Heath Closed.
Rayleigh (Eastwood Road Evangelical Church) 1923.

Rochford   (Rocheway) 1969
Romford   (Richmond Road Evangelical Church) 1933.
Shoebury   (West Road) 1932.
Silvertown   Closed.
Southend   (Milton Street) 1969.
South Green   Closed.
Stanford-le-Hope   (Victoria Road) 1924.
Stanway   (Chapel Road) 1886.
Steeple   Closed.
Tillingham   (South Street) 1897.
Totham   (Little Totham Evangelical Church, The Plains)
    1890.
Upchurch   (Kent) Closed.
Wakering, Great   (High Street) 1891.
Wakes Colne   Closed.
White Elm   Closed.
Wickford   (Nevendon Road) 1912.
Witham   (Guithavon Valley Evangelical Church) 1932.
Woodham Ferrers.   Closed.

Notes

CHAPTER ONE

1 An anonymous description quoted by Rev. Charles Herbert in 'An Essex Revival' (*Essex Review*) IV, 1895, pp. 37–44). No likeness of Banyard appears to have survived.

2 A Cruden's Concordance bearing James Banyard's signature and the date July 19th 1835, is in the possession of the Union of Evangelical Churches.

3 Israel Zangwill *Jinny the Carrier* (London 1919) p. 97.

4 Isaac Anderson *The Origin of the Peculiar People* (Southend 1882) p. 3.

5 Robert Aitken (1800–1873). He rejoined the Church of England in 1840. There is no evidence that he had any further contact with the Banyardites.

6 F. W. Harrod, who relates this episode in *The Peculiar People's Historical Jubilee Service* (Southend 1888) p. 6, continues: "Thus he (Layzell) continued to oppose him several times, publicly preaching against him, until he became very ill. He then expressed a desire to see Banyard, but his relatives would not allow him to be sent for, and although Banyard went to the house several times, asking permission to see him, Layzell's wife refused, and the young man died, whether within the twelve months and one day we cannot say. This we positively affirm – his life was very short and his comrade, Canum, died very soon after."

7 *Southend Standard* 24th May 1888. The Banyardite was Thomas Rayner of Great Wakering. In the same article, Rayner says that "He had not experienced the worst of it, but many times he had gone home scraping the slud out of his whiskers".

8 *The Origin of the Peculiar People* p. 5.

9 *The Peculiar People's Historical Jubilee Service* p. 11.

10 *A Life History of Isaac Anderson* (Southend 1896) p. 11, and *The Peculiar People's Historical Jubilee Service* p. 12. However, this is actually not the case. The Curate, Arthur R. Stert M.A., left the parish in 1849 to take up another appointment, the parishioners presenting him with a handsome silver salver for his charitable services. He returned to Prittlewell for a further term, leaving finally in 1863. "He was latterly a martyr to gout, and died suddenly in 1876, at Heatherby Place, Cheltenham, in his 66th year, leaving a widow and four children"

(Philip Benton *History of Rochford Hundred* II, p. 603.)

11   *The Peculiar People's Historical Jubilee Service* p. 13. That the early Banyardites wore the traditional Essex green smock is confirmed by the following extract from a speech given by an old Peculiar, Joseph Elsdon, at a Harvest Thanksgiving at Chelmsford in 1901: "It has been remarked that some of us know a little about poverty. I know a little. I have worked hard on a piece of bread, and I have worked hard for that. When I was in my prime I worked so hard I could not get upright to get a few pence for my family, but God has helped me . . . On Sundays, you know, when I was not altogether in poverty, but very low, I used to wear a long green smock, the poor man's Sunday dress. I hadn't a pair of shiny shoes (laughter) – but put on my old heavy high-deckers – you know, they used to call them that, they were 12 or 13 inches high – which I cleaned as well as I could on Saturday nights because I wished to go as tidy as I could to the House of the Lord on the Sabbath. I had not a nice pair of overalls to keep me from the wet, so my old master gave me an old pair of legging boots, off which I cut the bottoms, and so had the leggings, which I put under my trousers, as they were not tidy enough to be seen (laughter). But they kept me from the wet and so I was able to get to the House of God, which I did not want to miss. So I went, and they are my People today . . ."
Essex County Chronicle September 1901.

12   'Newlight' and 'Ranter' are both relics of 17th century religious controversies. In the 19th century, the Primitive Methodists were often so called, as in a bitter poem of John Clare's (written 1820–24) referring to their activities in Northamptonshire:

"Some turn from regular old forms as bad
To pious maniacs regularly mad,
A chosen race, so their conceit would teach,
Whom cant inspired to rave and not to preach,
A set of upstarts late from darkness sprung
With this new light, like mushrooms out of dung;
Tho' blind as owls i' the sun they lived before,
Conceit inspired and they are blind no more.
The drunken cobbler leaves his wicked life,
Hastes to save others, and neglects his wife;
To mend men's souls he thinks himself designed,
And leaves his shoes to the uncalled and blind;
He then like old songs runs the scriptures o'er
And makes discoveries never known before,
Makes darkest points as clear as ABC,
And wonders why his hearers will not see . . .
The Ranter priests, that take the street to teach,
Swear God builds churches whereso'er they preach . . ."
      The Parish: A Satire (Everyman ed. p. 147–8).

13   One whom Bridges' preaching inspired, was John Sirgood, who left London for Sussex in 1850, establishing at Loxwood a remarkable religious community known as the Cokelers or Society of Dependants with many resemblances to the Peculiar People. See John Montgo-

mery 'Abodes of Love' (London 1962); Earl Winterton 'The Cokelers: A Sussex Sect' ('Sussex County Magazine' November 1931, p. 717–722).

14 Punctuated as in the original. Banyard is buried in Rochford church-yard, on the south side near the wall.

CHAPTER TWO

1 A selection of these verses is to be found in Appendix II.
2 *The Times*, May 9, 1872. The Rev. C. Maurice Davies visited the area in April 1872, before Hurry's trial, and found that

> "The neighbourhood was literally up in arms against them – a fact on which I found the 'Peculiars' greatly prided themselves, as going to prove them in the coveted minority of the saints as opposed to the world. Were I to quote half the hard sayings which I gathered by diligent inquiry among the small shopkeepers and citizens in general, I should convert this article into a series of vituperations which I shall make it my business expressly to avoid. If unpopularity be a test of unsaintliness, the 'Peculiars' are certainly at the head of modern hagiology".

> *The Plumstead Peculiars* (Unorthodox London, 1874) p. 295.

3 In his one surviving sermon, (*Faith and Confidence in God: A Sermon by Mr D. Tansley* (not dated, but later than 1882), Tansley set out the argument for the Peculiars' stand on divine healing, as he saw it (p. 4–5):

> "People say that the Lord and physicians go together, but they do not go with me. Wordly reason and faith do not go together, but faith goes up to God for what is needed. Asa is reproached with having recourse unto the physicians rather than to the Lord. Thus it does not show in this case that physic and faith went together; it shows that in the earlier period there were physicians, but that their skill and practice were distinct from God's healing power. In the Gospels we read of some who sought unto physicians and spent all their substance, and were no better. They came unto the Lord, and He healed them. How did He do it? – 'thy faith hath made thee whole' . . . We give every man the opportunity to examine this matter, and he will find this virtue to be distinct from the physician's skill and his physics too.
> "It is often remarked of this healing in the Scriptures, that it has reference to the soul and not the body. Let our opponents have it so, and let us ask them if they get their souls healed. We shall find that they neither find the physician for the soul nor for the body. The soul is spoken of as diseased by sin, and the Scriptures show the soul to be made whole. Surely they ought to come at the one or the other. If they neither get the soul nor the body healed, then they must be outside this question. What are they then doing with the Scriptures? They just gather something to show them that they are miserable and sinful creatures. But, thank God, you and I have

had the healing balm, both for the soul and body, proving the healing of the body by faith correct, and the law of the Lord perfect, converting the soul . . ."

4   *The Times*, June 9, 1875; and *Punch*, June 19, 1875.

5   When this chapel at Daws Heath was demolished in 1976, a bottle lodged behind the façade was found to contain a note in Harrod's writing, giving the name of the chapel builder on the one side, and on the other the following:

"I do not lay this Stone thinking that it would
Consecrate the Place But as an acknowlegment
That it is for the use of the Peculiar People
Soley in the Name of God the Father God the
Son God the Holy Ghost
May Many Souls be Saved Here May Many
Bodyes be Healed Here & May its Walls
Long Echo to Gods Praise   *Amen*
S. Harrod April 7 1880".

6   But see the set of verses entitled 'The Thanksgiving', describing the Harvest Thanksgiving at Southend in 1881. Photograph on p. 49.

7   According to a report in *The Essex Chronicle* of September 1884, the numbers arriving for the meeting by rail, were as follows: London, 25; Woolwich, 40; Canning Town, 100; Witham, 90; Cressing, 85; Stanway, 56; Herongate, 60; Daws Heath and Hockley, 100; Stanford-le-Hope, 30. Contingents arrived by road from Tillingham, Steeple, Rochford, Southend, Foulness, Great Baddow, Wakering, and Ramsden Heath, and there were also members from Upchurch and other places in Kent.
The numbers of congregations noted in Bishop Harrod's own hand on a Plan of 1874–5, were as follows: Daws Heath, 59; London, 28; Herongate, 18; Woolwich, 18; Prittlewell, 48; Wakering, 18; White Elm, 9; Tillingham, 12; Steeple, 12; Foulness, 6; Witham, 30; Stanford, 30; Baddow, 12; Upchurch, 13; Canning Town, 48; Rivenhall (Cressing), 30: a total of 391. (See photograph on page 81.) Since then, estimates of numbers have varied widely; but it is doubtful if the total church at any time exceeded 5,000 members.

8   *Southend Standard* May 24, 1888.

9   The same. The *Essex Weekly News* May 25, 1888, gravely reports that provisions for tea on this occasion included 500 half-quartern loaves, 500 lbs of cake, 30 lbs of tea, 2½ cwt of sugar, 1½ cwt of butter, and 32 gallons of milk. Tea was apparently brewed in three boilers of 120,110 and 40 gallons respectively. Commemorative cups and saucers made for the occasion bear the inscription: 'Peculiar People's Jubilee, May 21st'.

10 *Essex Herald* September 24, 1889.

11 *Southend Standard* March 5, 1891.

12 *Article on Divine Healing* (Pamphlet 1900). The eight signatories of this document were George Brooks (London), Thomas Miller (Witham), W. Thorrington (Poplar), G. Nash (Woolwich), John Miller (Stanway), Walter Sachs (Southend, Lambert Street), Edward Brazier (Totham), and Joshua Hempstead (Grays). In the event, Sachs

alone did not join the Liberty Section.

CHAPTER THREE

1   *Essex County Chronicle* September 16, 1901; also *Essex Weekly News*
    September 23, 1904. Chignell continued: "My wages at one time of
    day were 12s. a week, and out of that it cost me close on 7s. for bread
    and flour, 2s. for rent, for I paid weekly. Seven shillings and two
    shillings make nine shillings, so there was not much left for extras
    after that, was there? . . ."
2   The same.
3   Special Council Meeting, 28 February 1910; Minute 646A (*Minute
    Book of The Peculiar People for Council and Council's Committee, January
    1903 – October 1938*).
4   This concession was arranged by Elder T. W. Moss of Rayleigh, who
    was also a local J.P., who continued to administer it until 1948, when
    the Approved Society was wound up, having been taken over under
    the National Health Act. According to a correspondent, it worked as
    follows:

> "One brother was appointed to care for our cards, to report when
> we were sick to the Elders – one of which used to visit us to see
> how sick we were – if off our feet and in bed, or couldn't work
> because of this sickness. We were paid a 'sickness benefit' which
> was far more than others outside got – after the Elder had put his
> signature to it . . ."

Even so, there was a certain oddness about this arrangement, for, as
my correspondent adds:

> "Of course, as you can guess, they didn't know what we were
> suffering from . . ."

5   Council's Committee Meeting, 11th April 1910; Minute 677 (*Minute
    Book* as above).
6   The same; Minute 674.
7   Apart from a continuing loyalty to the memory of Bishop Harrod,
    Paul Spicer and his followers failed to agree with Bishop Heddle's
    party on certain very minor doctrinal points, and particularly the
    wording of the 7th clause of the Deed Poll (see Note 8), objecting
    that the moral law is written in (not on) the heart etc. A new meeting
    place for the Original Peculiars was also built at Cressing by F. W.
    Scott in 1924. Here and at Prittlewell these last traditionalists of the
    Church could have been seen on a Sunday, dressed in strictest black,
    until very recent years; but they have now, I believe, almost entirely
    passed away.
8   These may be summarised as follows:

> (A) One living and true God; Three equally divine and distinct
> persons in the Godhead; Original sin; General redemption; Justifi-
> cation by faith in the death and resurrection of Christ alone; Regen-
> eration and Sanctification by the Spirit of God alone; That the law

of God (called the Moral) is written on the heart of believers and
they are called to obey it; The duty of all true believers to adopt a
life and conversation as becometh the Gospel of Christ in all true
believers; The resurrection of the body; The future judgement; The
eternal happiness of the righteous and the everlasting punishment
of such as die unforgiven.

(B) *Practices.* Baptism by sprinkling with water such only as are of
years of understanding upon their confession of repentance towards
God and faith in the atonement of and obedience to our Lord Jesus
Christ; Administration of the Lord's Supper to those who have
been so baptised; The laying on of hands and the anointing of oil
in the name of the Lord Jesus Christ for the healing of the sick
believing that God is the same yesterday, to-day and forever, and
that He can and does heal diseases in answer to the prayer of faith
without the aid of doctors or physic.

9   *Southend Telegraph* January 4, 1913.
10 *Southend Standard* January 9, 1913.
11 Although most of the congregation at the Original chapel on Daws
    Heath returned to the main church, the chapel itself, having been
    built specifically for Bishop Harrod and his party, remained in the
    hands of Paul Spicer. The Originals continued to worship here until
    just before the Second World War, when it was closed and sold.
12 *Rays of Light* No. 22, October 1914, p. 10.
13 Special Council Meeting, 31 January 1916; Minute 1288 (*Minute Book*).
14 Special Council Meeting, 15 May 1916; Minute 1319 (*Minute Book*).
    The Act received the Royal Assent on 25th May 1916.
15 I am indebted to Mr Hockley for this information.
16 Council Meeting, 7th April 1919; Minute 1560 (*Minute Book*).
17 *Re-Union Thanksgiving Services, held at Chelmsford, Essex, January 26th
    1921* (Pamphlet issued by 'Rays of Light' publishing committee) p.7.
18 The same p. 14.
19 Council Meeting, 3 April 1922; Minute 1777 (*Minute Book*).
20 Recommendation approved 2 October 1929 (*Minute Book*).
21 Council meeting, 11 January 1937: recommendations approved
    (*Minute Book*).

CHAPTER FOUR

1   *Rays of Light* No. 20, August 1914, p. 14.
2   *Rays of Light* No. 72, December 1918, p. 5–6.
3   *Rays of Light* No. 68, August 1918, p. 5.
4   *Rays of Light* No. 11, November 1913.
5   *The Peculiar People* (Pamphlet, Southend 1882). p 6. The Rector
    continues:

> "This I do know . . . that any one is at liberty to rise and tell about
> his past life, present troubles, and future prospects:– as, for instance,
> a man rises and says that in time past he has been a poacher, and
> a successful one, that he has now given it up, but has been troubled

what to do with a very clever dog, which he had trained, and which clung to old habits. Not being able to cure, he had just killed it. This and such-like stories, are received with loud 'Amens' – and stories of a more serious character, with loud 'Hallelujahs'. Young children are encouraged to assert their 'conversion' . . . This is very saddening . . ."

6   It is said that at cottage meetings, held in rotation at the houses of brethren living too far off to attend chapel, the brethren would sit in a circle for the same purpose of 'keeping out the Devil'.

7   Misuse of the Bible by preachers for sensational purposes was, naturally, very strongly disapproved. In the Minute Book, reference is made to "Bro. C's Visit to Daws Heath & the public reading of the 16th Chapter of Ezekiel & preaching therefrom & the effect of shame it brought over the congregation. It was also stated that the same scripture had been read by the same brother at S with the same effect". (Council's Committee Meeting, 5 October 1914, Minute 1170). Bishop Heddle was delegated to inform Bro. C. that the Council disapproved of the reading of such scriptures in public.

8   The one exception to this was the men who were in charge of animals on the farms. After considerable controversy, it was agreed that animals should be attended on Sundays at 8 o'clock in the morning, and 4 o'clock in the afternoon. Milking also had to be done: as one brother said, rather plaintively: "There's the milk: what are you going to do with it? You can't just pour it down the drain".

9   Quoted in *Abodes of Love* (London 1962) by John Montgomery.

10   *Rays of Light* No. 95, December 1920, p. 7.

11   *Rays of Light* No. 96, January 1921, p. 6. Also 'Rustic Comedy in Essex: Memories of . . . Great and Little Wakering' by Rev. Pendril Bentall in *Essex Countryside* No 181, February 1972.

12   *The Peculiar People* p. 31. A note attached to one copy of this pamphlet reads: "Bro. Jno Butcher got to know of Canon Bateman's pamphlet. Bros W. Heddle & Jno Brown wrote a letter to take with them to Canon Bateman, & a copy of the *original* pamphlet, telling C.B. that if this was issued in its present form they would proceed at law against him. C.B. said he had not authorised the sale of them. "We (Bros Heddle & Jno Brown) heard afterwards that after we had left, his coachman was directed to put the horse & carriage to & that he went & collected from the printer all the copies. Afterwards he had it issued in its altered form, by his authorisation & and not by ours, granpa told me this day 6/11/43."

13   *Rays of Light* No. 77, May 1919, p. 11.

14   *The Peculiar People*, pp. 15–18.

15   John Hockley manuscript p. 2 (see Appendix One).

16   *Essex Weekly News* September 30 1887.

CHAPTER FIVE

1   *Rays of Light* No. 23, November 1914, p. 11.

2   *Rays of Light* No. 6, June 1913.

3   *Rays of Light* No. 52, April 1917, p. 3.
4   The same.
5   *The Origin of the Peculiar People* (Southend 1882) p. 15.
6   *Rays of Light* No. 3, March 1913.
7   *Rays of Light* No. 4, April 1913.
8   *Rays of Light* No. 2, February 1913.
9   *Rays of Light* No. 107, December 1921, p. 4.
10 *Southend Standard* March 12, 1891. Brother Carey said this had happened "twenty-three years before".
11 I am indebted to Mr E. A. Barnes for this information.
12 *Rays of Light* No. 3, March 1913.
13 *Essex Herald* September 27, 1887.
14 *Rays of Light* No. 16, April 1914, p. 3.
15 *Essex Weekly News* September 16, 1912.
16 *Rays of Light* No. 4, April 1913. In a later form of her testimony the "strange form" of the vision becomes more specific: she chanced to look up to the ceiling:

> ". . . and there I saw what words cannot describe: I saw no distinct form, a bright mist seemed to veil the face, but all shone with a beautiful unearthly light – a light which did not seem to lighten anything else but centred on that strangely beautiful object from which it came, and then a voice told me not to be afraid" etc
> *In Memoriam. Exhorting Messages* by Florence J. Moss (née Philpot). (Booklet St. Albans 1942)

17 *Southend Standard* March 14, 1907, letter from George and Eliza Thorington: this is the same George Thorington who died at the Reunion thanksgiving in 1913. An independent account is given of one of the healings recorded here:

> "Chris Thorington was in the army when a horse reared and brought down his foot upon his skull smashing the forepart badly. In hospital nothing was accomplished, and for some years his life was a downright misery, with violent pains in the head continually.
> "The full story of his conversion he has given me over and over again: the casualness of his entry on the Sunday afternoon to the place of meeting of these Banyards, as they were called: the preacher, the text, the resistance in his mind, the groanings, the sighings, the pleadings by a lay sister, the yieldings, the conversion and the miracle.
> "What was the miracle?
> "Twenty-three pieces of bone came away next morning. Nineteen of these are to be seen today. The place from which they were taken – the front of the skull – showed always the mark of their departure. Yet there was no weakness. Chris was a market gardener, and ofttimes I have seen him carrying on his head large trays of vegetables of amazing weight . . ."
> *The Ancient Parish of Thundersley* by Rev E. A. B. Maley
> (Southend 1937), Chapter eleven.

Chris Thorington kept the fragments of bone in a tin, and used to

exhibit them to interested enquirers, living witnesses have seen them.
18 From an East London newspaper, July 1920. She was the widow of
    John Benton of Silvertown, who died in 1915.
19 "We the Peculiar People regard the promise in the 34th Psalm 20th
    verse 'He keepeth all his bones: not one of them is broken', as not
    being an exclusive prophesy & promise to the Saviour But a promise
    to all the truly righteous. And that the Lord Jesus Christ came fully
    heir thereto through him being absolutely righteous" (Special Council
    Meeting, 11 July 1917, Minute 1404). In 1886, Bishop Harrod rejoiced
    in the fact that he had heard of only two or three cases of broken
    limbs among the brethren since they assumed the title of 'peculiar' in
    1852. In 1887 he was even more dogmatic: "The Peculiar People did
    not meet with broken bones."
20 Sister Horsnell served her sentence at Holloway Prison, where she
    met many wealthy suffragettes, some of whom were on hunger
    strike. The rich hampers of food sent in for them by anxious relatives,
    which they refused, she was able to enjoy and partake of: it was much
    better food than she could ever get at home. The suffragettes asked
    her if she would join them: "No," she said, "I'm not in prison for
    that. I'm here for the death of my child".
21 Preface to *The Doctor's Dilemma* (Penguin, p. 11–12). See also a
    passing reference in the Preface to *St Joan* (Penguin p. 38)
22 *Southend Standard* April 18, 1907. A correspondent comments, regard-
    ing the use of medicines in general among the Peculiar People: "They
    believed in herbs of course; as one of the Elders said to me: 'There
    is much around growing, which God has provided for our use.'
    There is something in that, of course."
23 *Southend Standard* April 25, 1907. Ditto the following five extracts of
    evidence.
24 *Southend Standard* May 9, 1907. Ditto the following four extracts of
    speech.
25 *Essex Weekly News* June 21, 1907. Ditto the two following extracts
    of trial.

Bibliography

Anderson, Isaac, *The Origin of the Peculiar People* (Pamphlet, Southend 1882).

Anderson, Isaac, *The Life History of Isaac Anderson, A Member of the Peculiar People*. (Pamphlet, Southend 1896).

Anderson, Isaac, *Composed by Brother Isaac Anderson while afflicted on his bed* (Pamphlet, Southend 1910).

Bateman, Rev. Canon *The Peculiar People* (Pamphlet, Southend 1882).

Benton, Philip *History of Rochford Hundred* (Southend 1867–88).

Burrows, J. W. *Southend-on-Sea and District* (Southend 1909).

Davies, Rev. C. Maurice *Unorthodox London, or Phases of Religious Life in the Metropolis* (London 1874).

Harley, Laurence S. 'The "Peculiar People" – An Essex Sect' (*Essex Naturalist*, Vol 29, 1955; pp. 242–249).

Harrod, Frederick W. W. 'The Peculiar People's Historical Jubilee Service, written and compiled by F. W. Harrod from intelligence collected from S. Harrod and others' (Pamphlet, Southend 1888).

Harrod, Frederick W. W. *The Centenary of the Peculiar People 1838–1938* (Pamphlet, Southend 1938).

Hayward, Rev. Thomas *Essex Congregational Magazine* (March 1868).

Heddle, William *A brief account of my Life and Experience* (Pamphlet, Southend 1930).

Herbert, Rev. Charles 'An Essex Revival' (*Essex Review* IV, 1895, pp. 37–44).

Montgomery, John *Abodes of Love* (London 1962).

Young, Kenneth *Chapel, the joyous days and prayerful nights of the Nonconformists in their heyday circa 1850–1950* (London 1972).

Heddle, Wm. and Others. Rays of Light (Southend 1913–

1928). A magazine issued monthly by the Peculiar People.

Harrod, S. and others. *The Peculiar People's Hymn Book.* Selected from various sources by S. Harrod, D. Handley, and W. Lewin . . . published and sold by D. Handley and S. Harrod, Maldon Essex 1860'. (Additions and revisions 1867, 1880, 1910 etc).

Jiggens, Fred J. *Glory Be* (Arthur H. Stockwell Ltd. Ilfracombe 1978)

Index